NINJA WOODFIRE ELECTRIC

BBQ Grill & Smoker Cookbook

for Beginners

2000 Days of Easy, Mouth-Watering Recipes for Outdoor Grilling, BBQ, Bake, Roast, Dehydrate, Discover More Grilling Fun By Tips

Eve Wilkinson

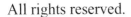

Welcome to the world of [Eve Wilkinson]'s culinary creations! We're thrilled to share our love for food through this recipe book, but before you start your culinary adventure, please take a moment to familiarize yourself with our copyright statement and disclaimer, which outline the guidelines for using this book.

Cooking is a wonderful journey, but it's important to be aware of potential hazards. While we've taken every care to provide accurate and safe recipes, individual results may vary. We assume no responsibility for any accidents, injuries, or allergies that may occur while using this book. Exercise caution, follow food safety guidelines, and consult professionals as needed.

Thank you for choosing [Eve Wilkinson]'s [Ninja Woodfire Electric BBQ Grill & Smoker Cookbook for Beginners]. Your support is deeply appreciated, and we hope these recipes enrich your culinary experiences.

A super simple, easy and delicious collection of outdoor grilling recipes

Easy tips for grilling and cooking to perfection

Cleanup Tips for Electric BBQ Grill & Smoker

It's not just grilling, it's baking, frying ....

CONTENTS

INTRODUCTION

Hi there, I'm Eve Wilkinson, and I'm thrilled to unveil the essence of smoky, sizzling goodness with the Ninja Woodfire Electric BBQ Grill & Smoker Cookbook. My journey to this cookbook emerged from a lifetime of culinary passion coupled with a professional pursuit in the world of flavors. With a background in crafting delightful culinary experiences and a fervor for all things BBQ, I've carefully curated a cookbook that isn't just a collection of recipes but a roadmap to mastering the art of grilling and smoking.

The purpose behind penning this cookbook was simple - to demystify the sometimes-intimidating world of grilling and smoking and make it as accessible and enjoyable as a walk in the park. Each recipe isn't just a set of steps; it's a story, a journey, and a promise. With step-by-step instructions, bonus do-it-yourself (DIY) tips, and meticulously curated shopping lists, I want to ensure that the process of grilling and smoking is not just about the outcome but about the delightful experience. And because I know the modern-day whirlwind, I've thrown in estimated cooking times and practical tips to make grilling and smoking not just a culinary adventure, but a doable, achievable daily delight.

So, whether you're a grilling aficionado or a newbie just starting your BBQ adventure, my aim with this cookbook is simple: to invite you to savor not just the flavors but the entire journey. This is your personal invitation to a world where the tantalizing aroma of BBQ isn't just a distant dream but a flavorful reality. Welcome to the exciting, smoky, and flavor-rich world of Eve Wilkinson's Ninja Woodfire Electric BBQ Grill & Smoker Cookbook. Let the culinary magic begin!

WHAT IS NINJA WOODFIRE ELECTRIC BBQ GRILL & SMOKER?

The Ninja Woodfire Electric BBQ Grill & Smoker is a multifunctional kitchen appliance that offers the convenience of indoor grilling and smoking without the need for an outdoor setup. It is equipped with multiple cooking functions that allow users to grill, air dry, roast, bake, dehydrate, and smoke food for a variety of flavors and textures. The unit uses a combination of heating elements and a built-in fan to deliver precise and adjustable heat for consistent grilling or smoking temperatures. The Smart Cooking System offers programmable settings and a variety of preset options for flexibility and ease of use. This Ninja Foodi grill and smoker accommodates a variety of cooking styles for those who enjoy the convenience of indoor grilling and smoking without sacrificing flavor.

WHAT ARE THE ADVANTAGES OF NINJA WOODFIRE ELECTRIC BBQ GRILL & SMOKER?

VERSATILITY

This appliance offers a wide range of cooking options, allowing you to grill, smoke, air crisp, roast, bake, and dehydrate food. Its multi-functionality provides diverse cooking methods in a single device, catering to various culinary preferences.

INDOOR CONVENIENCE

The Ninja Foodi Grill allows users to enjoy the experience of grilling and smoking indoors, bypassing the limitations or restrictions of outdoor setups. It's ideal for those living in apartments, areas with limited outdoor space, or during inclement weather conditions.

PRECISE COOKING

The Smart Cook System enables precise control over cooking temperatures and times, allowing users to achieve consistent and tailored results. Programmable settings and pre-set options simplify the cooking process for precise outcomes.

EASE OF USE

With intuitive controls and programmable settings, the appliance is user-friendly and accessible to both experienced cooks and beginners. The pre-set options streamline the cooking process, reducing the guesswork in achieving desired cooking results.

SPACE-EFFICIENT DESIGN

By combining multiple cooking functions in one appliance, it helps save kitchen space by reducing the need for separate devices dedicated to grilling, smoking, roasting, and other functions.

FLAVORFUL RESULTS

The smoker function infuses foods with a rich, smoky flavor, adding an extra dimension to dishes without the need for an outdoor smoker. This feature caters to those seeking the taste of smoked foods without the outdoor setup.

EASE OF CLEANING

Many components, such as the grill grate and cooking pot, are dishwasher safe, simplifying the cleaning process. The removable parts make cleanup relatively hassle-free, enhancing the overall user experience.

HOW TO CLEAN NINJA WOODFIRE ELECTRIC BBQ GRILL & SMOKER?

Cool Down: Ensure the grill has cooled down completely before starting the cleaning process to avoid burns.

Remove Parts: Take out removable components such as the grill grate, cooking pot, and any other detachable parts.

Wash Removable Parts: Wash the detachable parts with warm, soapy water. Use a non-abrasive sponge or cloth to clean off any food residue. Some parts might be dishwasher safe, so check the user manual for specific instructions.

Clean the Hood: Wipe down the interior and exterior of the hood using a damp cloth or sponge. Avoid using abrasive cleaners that could damage the surface.

Clean the Drip Tray: Empty and clean the drip tray. If there are any stubborn stains or grease, use warm, soapy water and a sponge to remove them.

Check for Grease Buildup: If there's grease or residue built up on the heating element or other areas, use a damp cloth to wipe them clean. Avoid using excessive water or harsh cleaning products on electrical components.

Dry and Reassemble: Ensure all the components are completely dry before reassembling the grill. Once dry, reassemble the grill and return all the parts to their respective places.

BREAKFASTST

Grilled Sausage Mix

Servings: 4 | Cooking Time: 22 Minutes

Ingredients:
- 8 mini bell peppers
- 2 heads radicchio, each cut into 6 wedges
- Canola oil, for brushing
- Sea salt, to taste
- Freshly ground black pepper, to taste
- 6 breakfast sausage links
- 6 hot or sweet Italian sausage links

Directions:
1. Insert the Grill Grate and close the hood. Select GRILL, set the temperature to MAX, and set the time to 22 minutes. Select START/STOP to begin preheating.
2. While the unit is preheating, brush the bell peppers and radicchio with the oil. Season with salt and black pepper.
3. When the unit beeps to signify it has preheated, place the bell peppers and radicchio on the Grill Grate; close the hood and GRILL for 10 minutes, without flipping.
4. Meanwhile, poke the sausages with a fork or knife and brush them with some of the oil.
5. After 10 minutes, remove the vegetables and set aside. Decrease the temperature to LOW. Place the sausages on the Grill Grate; close the hood and GRILL for 6 minutes.
6. Flip the sausages. Close the hood and GRILL for 6 minutes more. Remove the sausages from the Grill Grate.
7. Serve the sausages and vegetables on a large cutting board or serving tray.

Cream Cheese–stuffed French Toast

Servings: 6 | Cooking Time: 6 Minutes

Ingredients:
- 2 large eggs
- 1 cup milk
- 1 teaspoon cinnamon
- 1 teaspoon light brown sugar, packed
- 1 teaspoon vanilla extract
- 1 (8-ounce) package whipped cream cheese (flavored or plain)
- 12 slices white bread

Directions:
1. Insert the Grill Grate and close the hood. Select GRILL, set the temperature to HI, and set the time to 6 minutes. Select START/STOP to begin preheating.
2. While the unit is preheating, in a small bowl, whisk together the eggs, milk, cinnamon, brown sugar, and vanilla.
3. Spread a thick layer of cream cheese on one side of 6 bread slices. Top each with the remaining 6 bread slices. Dip the sandwich into the egg mixture, making sure to coat both sides completely.
4. When the unit beeps to signify it has preheated, place the French toast sandwiches on the Grill Grate. Close the hood and grill for 3 minutes.
5. After 3 minutes, open the hood and flip the French toast. Close the hood and continue cooking for 3 minutes more.
6. When cooking is complete, remove the French toast from the grill and serve.

Servings: 4 | Cooking Time: 23 Minutes

Ingredients:

- 1 package ground breakfast sausage, crumbled
- 3 large eggs, lightly beaten
- ⅓ cup diced red bell pepper
- ⅓ cup thinly sliced scallions (green part only)
- Sea salt, to taste
- Freshly ground black pepper, to taste
- 1 package pizza dough
- All-purpose flour, for dusting
- 1 cup shredded Cheddar cheese
- 2 tablespoons canola oil

Directions:

1. Select ROAST, set the temperature to 375ºF, and set the time to 15 minutes. Select START/STOP to begin preheating.

2. When the unit beeps to signify it has preheated, place the sausage directly in the pot. Close the hood, and ROAST for 10 minutes, checking the sausage every 2 to 3 minutes, breaking apart larger pieces with a wooden spoon.

3. After 10 minutes, pour the eggs, bell pepper, and scallions into the pot. Stir to evenly incorporate with the sausage. Close the hood and let the eggs roast for the remaining 5 minutes, stirring occasionally. Transfer the sausage and egg mixture to a medium bowl to cool slightly. Season with salt and pepper.

4. Insert the Crisper Basket and close the hood. Select AIR CRISP, set the temperature to 350ºF, and set the time to 8 minutes. Select START/STOP to begin preheating.

5. Meanwhile, divide the dough into four equal pieces. Lightly dust a clean work surface with flour. Roll each piece of dough into a 5-inch round of even thickness. Divide the sausage-egg mixture and cheese evenly among each round. Brush the outside edge of the dough with water. Fold the dough over the filling, forming a half circle. Pinch the edges of the dough together to seal in the filling. Brush both sides of each pocket with the oil.

6. When the unit beeps to signify it has preheated, place the breakfast pockets in the basket. Close the hood and AIR CRISP for 6 to 8 minutes, or until golden brown.

Avocado Eggs

Servings: 4 | Cooking Time: 10 Minutes

Ingredients:

- 4 ripe avocados, divided
- 3 tablespoons extra-virgin olive oil
- 1 teaspoon salt
- ½ teaspoon freshly ground black pepper
- 8 small eggs
- Hot sauce or salsa, for garnish (optional)

Directions:

1. Insert the Grill Grate and close the hood. Select GRILL, set the temperature to HI, and set the time to 10 minutes. Select START/STOP to begin preheating.

2. While the unit is preheating, cut the avocados in half lengthwise and remove the pits, but leave the skin on. You may need to scoop out some of the green flesh so the egg fits once added. Set the extra flesh aside to use as an additional topping later.

3. In a small bowl, whisk together the olive oil, salt, and pepper. Brush the seasoned olive oil on the flesh of the avocados. Then, crack an egg into the center of each avocado half.

4. When the unit beeps to signify it has preheated, place the avocados on the grill, egg-side up. Close the hood and grill for 10 minutes.

5. Cooking is complete when the egg whites are firm. Remove the avocados from the grill. Garnish with the reserved avocado and top with your favorite hot sauce or salsa, if desired.

Bacon And Egg Bread Cups

Servings: 4 | Cooking Time: 8 To 12 Minutes

Ingredients:

- 4 crusty rolls
- 4 thin slices Gouda or Swiss cheese mini wedges
- 5 eggs
- 2 tablespoons heavy cream
- 3 strips precooked bacon, chopped
- ½ teaspoon dried thyme
- Pinch salt
- Freshly ground black pepper, to taste

Directions:

1. Select BAKE, set the temperature to 330ºF, and set the time to 12 minutes. Select START/STOP to begin pre-heating.
2. On a clean work surface, cut the tops off the rolls. Using your fingers, remove the insides of the rolls to make bread cups, leaving a ½-inch shell. Place a slice of cheese onto each roll bottom.
3. Whisk together the eggs and heavy cream in a medium bowl until well combined. Fold in the bacon, thyme, salt, and pepper and stir well.
4. Scrape the egg mixture into the prepared bread cups.
5. Place the bread cups directly in the pot. Close the hood and BAKE for 8 to 12 minutes, or until the eggs are cooked to your preference.
6. Serve warm.

Pb&j

Servings: 4 | Cooking Time: 6 Minutes

Ingredients:

- ½ cup cornflakes, crushed
- ¼ cup shredded coconut
- 8 slices oat nut bread or any whole-grain, oversize bread
- 6 tablespoons peanut butter
- 2 medium bananas, cut into ½-inch-thick slices
- 6 tablespoons pineapple preserves
- 1 egg, beaten
- Cooking spray

Directions:

1. Insert the Crisper Basket and close the hood. Select AIR CRISP, set the temperature to 360ºF, and set the time to 6 minutes. Select START/STOP to begin preheating.
2. In a shallow dish, mix the cornflake crumbs and coconut.
3. For each sandwich, spread one bread slice with 1½ tablespoons of peanut butter. Top with banana slices. Spread another bread slice with 1½ tablespoons of preserves. Combine to make a sandwich.
4. Using a pastry brush, brush top of sandwich lightly with beaten egg. Sprinkle with about 1½ tablespoons of crumb coating, pressing it in to make it stick. Spray with cooking spray.
5. Turn sandwich over and repeat to coat and spray the other side. Place the sandwiches in the Crisper Basket.
6. Close the hood and AIR CRISP for 6 minutes or until coating is golden brown and crispy.
7. Cut the cooked sandwiches in half and serve warm.

Servings: 2 | Cooking Time: 20 To 23 Minutes

Ingredients:
- 4 large eggs
- 4 ounces baby bella mushrooms, chopped
- 1 cup baby spinach, chopped
- ½ cup shredded Cheddar cheese
- ⅓ cup chopped leek, white part only
- ¼ cup halved grape tomatoes
- 1 tablespoon 2% milk
- ¼ teaspoon dried oregano
- ¼ teaspoon garlic powder
- ½ teaspoon kosher salt
- Freshly ground black pepper, to taste
- Cooking spray

Directions:

1. Select BAKE, set the temperature to 300°F, and set the time to 23 minutes. Select START/STOP to begin pre-heating.
2. Lightly spritz a baking pan with cooking spray.
3. Whisk the eggs in a large bowl until frothy. Add the mushrooms, baby spinach, cheese, leek, tomatoes, milk, oregano, garlic powder, salt, and pepper and stir until well blended. Pour the mixture into the prepared baking pan.
4. Place the pan directly in the pot. Close the hood and BAKE for 20 to 23 minutes, or until the center is puffed up and the top is golden brown.
5. Let the frittata cool for 5 minutes before slicing to serve.

Honey-lime Glazed Grilled Fruit Salad

Servings: 4 | Cooking Time: 4 Minutes

Ingredients:
- ½ pound strawberries, washed, hulled and halved
- 1 can pineapple chunks, drained, juice reserved
- 2 peaches, pitted and sliced
- 6 tablespoons honey, divided
- 1 tablespoon freshly squeezed lime juice

Directions:

1. Insert the Grill Grate and close the hood. Select GRILL, set the temperature to MAX, and set the time to 4 minutes. Select START/STOP to begin preheating.
2. While the unit is preheating, combine the strawberries, pineapple, and peaches in a large bowl with 3 tablespoons of honey. Toss to coat evenly.
3. When the unit beeps to signify it has preheated, place the fruit on the Grill Grate. Gently press the fruit down to maximize grill marks. Close the hood and GRILL for 4 minutes without flipping.
4. Meanwhile, in a small bowl, combine the remaining 3 tablespoons of honey, lime juice, and 1 tablespoon of reserved pineapple juice.
5. When cooking is complete, place the fruit in a large bowl and toss with the honey mixture. Serve immediately.

Spinach Omelet

Servings: 1 | Cooking Time: 10 Minutes

Ingredients:
- 1 teaspoon olive oil
- 3 eggs
- Salt and ground black pepper, to taste
- 1 tablespoon ricotta cheese
- ¼ cup chopped spinach
- 1 tablespoon chopped parsley

Directions:
1. Grease a baking pan with olive oil.
2. Select BAKE, set the temperature to 330ºF, and set the time to 10 minutes. Select START/STOP to begin pre-heating.
3. In a bowl, beat the eggs with a fork and sprinkle salt and pepper.
4. Add the ricotta, spinach, and parsley and then transfer to the baking pan. Place the pan directly in the pot.
5. Close the hood and BAKE for 10 minutes or until the egg is set.
6. Serve warm.

Spinach With Scrambled Eggs

Servings: 2 | Cooking Time: 10 Minutes

Ingredients:
- 2 tablespoons olive oil
- 4 eggs, whisked
- 5 ounces fresh spinach, chopped
- 1 medium tomato, chopped
- 1 teaspoon fresh lemon juice
- ½ teaspoon coarse salt
- ½ teaspoon ground black pepper
- ½ cup of fresh basil, roughly chopped

Directions:
1. Grease a baking pan with the oil, tilting it to spread the oil around.
2. Select BAKE, set the temperature to 280ºF, and set the time to 10 minutes. Select START/STOP to begin pre-heating.
3. In the pan, mix the remaining ingredients, apart from the basil leaves, whisking well until everything is completely combined.
4. Place the pan directly in the pot. Close the hood and BAKE for 10 minutes.
5. Top with fresh basil leaves before serving.

Western Omelet

Servings: 2 | Cooking Time: 18 To 21 Minutes

Ingredients:
- ¼ cup chopped bell pepper, green or red
- ¼ cup chopped onion
- ¼ cup diced ham
- 1 teaspoon butter
- 4 large eggs
- 2 tablespoons milk
- ⅛ teaspoon salt
- ¾ cup shredded sharp Cheddar cheese

Directions:
1. Select AIR CRISP, set the temperature to 390°F, and set the time to 6 minutes. Select START/STOP to begin preheating.
2. Put the bell pepper, onion, ham, and butter in a baking pan and mix well. Place the pan directly in the pot.
3. Close the hood and AIR CRISP for 1 minute. Stir and continue to cook for an additional 4 to 5 minutes until the veggies are softened.
4. Meanwhile, whisk together the eggs, milk, and salt in a bowl.
5. Pour the egg mixture over the veggie mixture.
6. Reduce the grill temperature to 360°F and BAKE for 13 to 15 minutes more, or until the top is lightly golden browned and the eggs are set.
7. Scatter the omelet with the shredded cheese. Bake for another 1 minute until the cheese has melted.
8. Let the omelet cool for 5 minutes before serving.

Tomato-corn Frittata With Avocado Dressing

Servings: 2 Or 3 | Cooking Time: 20 Minutes

Ingredients:
- ½ cup cherry tomatoes, halved
- Kosher salt and freshly ground black pepper, to taste
- 6 large eggs, lightly beaten
- ½ cup corn kernels, thawed if frozen
- ¼ cup milk
- 1 tablespoon finely chopped fresh dill
- ½ cup shredded Monterey Jack cheese
- Avocado Dressing:
- 1 ripe avocado, pitted and peeled
- 2 tablespoons fresh lime juice
- ¼ cup olive oil
- 1 scallion, finely chopped
- 8 fresh basil leaves, finely chopped

Directions:
1. Put the tomato halves in a colander and lightly season with salt. Set aside for 10 minutes to drain well. Pour the tomatoes into a large bowl and fold in the eggs, corn, milk, and dill. Sprinkle with salt and pepper and stir until mixed.
2. Select BAKE, set the temperature to 300°F, and set the time to 20 minutes. Select START/STOP to begin pre-heating.
3. Pour the egg mixture into a baking pan. Place the pan directly in the pot. Close the hood and BAKE for 15 minutes.
4. Scatter the cheese on top. Increase the grill temperature to 315°F and continue to cook for another 5 minutes, or until the frittata is puffy and set.
5. Meanwhile, make the avocado dressing: Mash the avocado with the lime juice in a medium bowl until smooth. Mix in the olive oil, scallion, and basil and stir until well incorporated.
6. Let the frittata cool for 5 minutes and serve alongside the avocado dressing.

Crustless Broccoli Quiche

Servings: 4 | Cooking Time: 10 Minutes

Ingredients:

- 1 cup broccoli florets
- ¾ cup chopped roasted red peppers
- 1¼ cups grated Fontina cheese
- 6 eggs
- ¾ cup heavy cream
- ½ teaspoon salt
- Freshly ground black pepper, to taste
- Cooking spray

Directions:

1. Select AIR CRISP, set the temperature to 325°F, and set the time to 10 minutes. Select START/STOP to begin preheating.
2. Spritz a baking pan with cooking spray
3. Add the broccoli florets and roasted red peppers to the pan and scatter the grated Fontina cheese on top.
4. In a bowl, beat together the eggs and heavy cream. Sprinkle with salt and pepper. Pour the egg mixture over the top of the cheese. Wrap the pan in foil.
5. Place the pan directly in the pot. Close the hood and AIR CRISP for 8 minutes. Remove the foil and continue to cook another 2 minutes until the quiche is golden brown.
6. Rest for 5 minutes before cutting into wedges and serve warm.

Stuffed Bell Peppers With Italian Maple-glazed Sausage

Servings: 6 | Cooking Time: 28 Minutes

Ingredients:

- 2 pounds ground Italian sausage or links
- 1 cup light brown sugar, packed
- 6 bell peppers (any color)
- 1 cup water
- 12 tablespoons (¾ cup) maple syrup, divided

Directions:

1. Insert the Cooking Pot and close the hood. Select GRILL, set the temperature to HI, and set the time to 8 minutes. Select START/STOP to begin preheating.
2. While the unit is preheating, remove the sausage from the casings if using links.
3. When the unit beeps to signify it has preheated, place the sausage and brown sugar in the Cooking Pot. Use a wooden spoon or potato masher to break the sausage apart and mix it with the brown sugar. Close the hood and cook for 8 minutes.
4. While the sausage is cooking, cut the top off each bell pepper and remove the seeds. Then slice the bell peppers in half lengthwise.
5. When cooking is complete, spoon the sausage into each bell pepper cup. Add the water to the Cooking Pot. Place 6 bell pepper halves on the Grill Grate, and place the Grill Grate in the unit.
6. Select GRILL, set the temperature to HI, and set the time to 20 minutes. Select START/STOP and then press the PREHEAT button to skip preheating. Close the hood and cook for 5 minutes.
7. After 5 minutes, open the hood and drizzle 1 tablespoon of maple syrup in each bell pepper cup. Close the hood and cook 5 minutes more. After 5 minutes, remove the stuffed peppers and place the remaining 6 stuffed peppers on the Grill Grate. Repeat this step to cook.
8. When cooking is complete, remove the peppers from the grill and serve.
9. Adding raw sausage inside a bell pepper will result in a watery mess.

Servings: 4 | Cooking Time: 8 Minutes

Ingredients:
- 4 large eggs
- 4 croissants
- 8 tablespoons pesto

Directions:
1. Insert the Cooking Pot and close the hood. Select GRILL, set the temperature to HI, and set the time to 8 minutes. Select START/STOP to begin preheating.
2. While the unit is preheating, in a small bowl, whisk together the eggs.
3. When the unit beeps to signify it has preheated, pour the beaten eggs into the Cooking Pot. Close the hood and cook for 4 minutes.
4. While the eggs are cooking, split the croissants. Place the croissant halves on top of the Grill Grate.
5. After 4 minutes, open the hood and scramble the eggs with a spatula. Spoon the scrambled eggs onto the bottom halves of the croissants. Remove the Cooking Pot from the unit.
6. Insert the Grill Grate into the unit. Spoon 2 tablespoons of pesto on top of each egg-topped croissant, then top each sandwich with the croissant top. Close the hood and cook for 4 minutes.
7. When cooking is complete, the croissant crust should be toasted. Serve.

Avocado Quesadillas

Servings: 4 | Cooking Time: 11 Minutes

Ingredients:
- 4 eggs
- 2 tablespoons skim milk
- Salt and ground black pepper, to taste
- Cooking spray
- 4 flour tortillas
- 4 tablespoons salsa
- 2 ounces Cheddar cheese, grated
- ½ small avocado, peeled and thinly sliced

Directions:
1. Select BAKE, set the temperature to 270°F, and set the time to 8 minutes. Select START/STOP to begin preheating.
2. Beat together the eggs, milk, salt, and pepper.
3. Spray a baking pan lightly with cooking spray and add egg mixture.
4. Place the pan directly in the pot. Close the hood and BAKE for 8 minutes, stirring every 1 to 2 minutes, until eggs are scrambled to the liking. Remove and set aside.
5. Spray one side of each tortilla with cooking spray. Flip over.
6. Divide eggs, salsa, cheese, and avocado among the tortillas, covering only half of each tortilla.
7. Fold each tortilla in half and press down lightly. Increase the temperature of the grill to 390°F.
8. Put 2 tortillas in Crisper Basket and AIR CRISP for 3 minutes or until cheese melts and outside feels slightly crispy. Repeat with remaining two tortillas.
9. Cut each cooked tortilla into halves. Serve warm.

Cheesy Breakfast Casserole

Servings: 4 | Cooking Time: 14 Minutes

Ingredients:
- 6 slices bacon
- 6 eggs
- Salt and pepper, to taste
- Cooking spray
- ½ cup chopped green bell pepper
- ½ cup chopped onion
- ¾ cup shredded Cheddar cheese

Directions:
1. Place the bacon in a skillet over medium-high heat and cook each side for about 4 minutes until evenly crisp. Remove from the heat to a paper towel-lined plate to drain. Crumble it into small pieces and set aside.
2. Whisk the eggs with the salt and pepper in a medium bowl.
3. Select BAKE, set the temperature to 400ºF, and set the time to 8 minutes. Select START/STOP to begin pre-heating.
4. Spritz a baking pan with cooking spray.
5. Place the whisked eggs, crumbled bacon, green bell pepper, and onion in the prepared pan. Place the pan directly in the pot. Close the hood and BAKE for 6 minutes.
6. Scatter the Cheddar cheese all over and bake for 2 minutes more.
7. Allow to sit for 5 minutes and serve on plates.

Cinnamon Sugar Roll-ups

Servings: 4 | Cooking Time: 10 Minutes

Ingredients:
- 1 sheet frozen puff pastry, thawed
- 3 tablespoons cinnamon
- 5 tablespoons granulated sugar
- 2 tablespoons unsalted butter, melted, divided

Directions:
1. Insert the Grill Grate and close the hood. Select GRILL, set the temperature to LO, and set the time to 10 minutes. Select START/STOP to begin preheating.
2. While the unit is preheating, unroll the pastry dough on a flat surface. In a small bowl, combine the cinnamon and the sugar. Brush 1 tablespoon of butter over the surface of the pastry. Then sprinkle on the cinnamon sugar evenly.
3. Carefully roll the pastry into a log. Using a sharp knife, cut the log into 1- to 2-inch slices. Lightly brush the top and bottom of the roll-ups with the remaining 1 tablespoon of butter.
4. When the unit beeps to signify it has preheated, place the roll-ups on the Grill Grate. Close the hood and grill for 5 minutes.
5. After 5 minutes, open the hood and flip the roll-ups. Close the hood and cook for 5 minutes more.
6. When cooking is complete, the roll-ups will be a nice golden brown. Serve.

Supersized Family Pizza Omelet

Servings: 4 | Cooking Time: 10 Minutes

Ingredients:
- 10 large eggs
- 1 tablespoon Italian seasoning
- ½ cup pizza or marinara sauce
- 1 cup shredded mozzarella cheese
- 2 ounces pepperoni slices (about 24 slices)

Directions:
1. Insert the Cooking Pot and close the hood. Select GRILL, set the temperature to HI, and set the time to 10 minutes. Select START/STOP to begin preheating.
2. While the unit is preheating, in a medium bowl, whisk together the eggs and Italian seasoning.
3. When the unit beeps to signify it has preheated, pour the egg mixture into the Cooking Pot. Close the hood and cook for 5 minutes.
4. Place the Grill Grate next to the unit on top of the counter. After 5 minutes, open the hood and use a spatula to fold the egg sheet in half, then place it on top of the Grill Grate.
5. Place the Grill Grate into the unit. Top the omelet with the pizza sauce, mozzarella cheese, and pepperoni slices. Close the hood and cook for 5 minutes more.
6. When cooking is complete, the cheese will be melted. Remove the omelet from the grill and serve.

Brie And Apple Tart

Servings: 4 | Cooking Time: 10 Minutes

Ingredients:
- 1 sheet ready-to-bake puff pastry (thawed, if frozen)
- 1 small apple, cored and thinly sliced
- 3 tablespoons honey
- 1 teaspoon light brown sugar, packed
- 1 (8-ounce) round Brie cheese
- 2 tablespoons unsalted butter, melted

Directions:
1. Insert the Grill Grate and close the hood. Select GRILL, set the temperature to LO, and set the time to 10 minutes. Select START/STOP to begin preheating.
2. While the unit is preheating, unroll the pastry dough on a flat surface. Place the apple slices in the center of the dough. Drizzle the honey over the apples and sprinkle the brown sugar on top. Unwrap the Brie and place it on top of the apple slices. Fold the ends of the pastry around the Brie, similar to wrapping up a package, making sure to fully enclose the Brie and apples. Using a basting brush, brush the pastry all over with the melted butter.
3. When the unit beeps to signify it has preheated, place the pastry on the grill. Close the hood and grill for 10 minutes.
4. When cooking is complete, the pastry will be a nice golden brown. The Brie may leak out while cooking, and this is okay. The filling will be hot, so be sure to let it cool for a few minutes before serving.

Servings: 4 | Cooking Time: 10 Minutes

Ingredients:

- 1 can full-fat coconut milk, refrigerated overnight
- ½ tablespoon powdered sugar
- 1½ teaspoons vanilla extract, divided
- 1 cup halved strawberries
- 1 tablespoon maple syrup, plus more for garnish
- 1 tablespoon brown sugar, divided
- ¾ cup lite coconut milk
- 2 large eggs
- ½ teaspoon ground cinnamon
- 2 tablespoons unsalted butter, at room temperature
- 4 slices challah bread

Directions:

1. Turn the chilled can of full-fat coconut milk upside down (do not shake the can), open the bottom, and pour out the liquid coconut water. Scoop the remaining solid coconut cream into a medium bowl. Using an electric hand mixer, whip the cream for 3 to 5 minutes, until soft peaks form.

2. Add the powdered sugar and ½ teaspoon of the vanilla to the coconut cream, and whip it again until creamy. Place the bowl in the refrigerator.

3. Insert the Grill Grate and close the hood. Select GRILL, set the temperature to MAX, and set the time to 15 minutes. Select START/STOP to begin preheating.

4. While the unit is preheating, combine the strawberries with the maple syrup and toss to coat evenly. Sprinkle evenly with ½ tablespoon of the brown sugar.

5. In a large shallow bowl, whisk together the lite coconut milk, eggs, the remaining 1 teaspoon of vanilla, and cinnamon.

6. When the unit beeps to signify it has preheated, place the strawberries on the Grill Grate. Gently press the fruit down to maximize grill marks. Close the hood and GRILL for 4 minutes without flipping.

7. Meanwhile, butter each slice of bread on both sides. Place one slice in the egg mixture and let it soak for 1 minute. Flip the slice over and soak it for another minute. Repeat with the remaining bread slices. Sprinkle each side of the toast with the remaining ½ tablespoon of brown sugar.

8. After 4 minutes, remove the strawberries from the grill and set aside. Decrease the temperature to HIGH. Place the bread on the Grill Grate; close the hood and GRILL for 4 to 6 minutes until golden and caramelized. Check often to ensure desired doneness.

9. Place the toast on a plate and top with the strawberries and whipped coconut cream. Drizzle with maple syrup, if desired.

SIDES, SNACKS & APPETIZERS

Garlicky And Lemony Artichokes

Servings: 4 | Cooking Time: 10 Minutes

Ingredients:
- Juice of ½ lemon
- ½ cup canola oil
- 3 garlic cloves, chopped
- Sea salt, to taste
- Freshly ground black pepper, to taste
- 2 large artichokes, trimmed and halved

Directions:
1. Insert the Grill Grate and close the hood. Select GRILL, set the temperature to MAX, and set the time to 10 minutes. Select START/STOP to begin preheating.
2. While the unit is preheating, in a medium bowl, combine the lemon juice, oil, and garlic. Season with salt and pepper, then brush the artichoke halves with the lemon-garlic mixture.
3. When the unit beeps to signify it has preheated, place the artichokes on the Grill Grate, cut side down. Gently press them down to maximize grill marks. Close the hood and GRILL for 8 to 10 minutes, occasionally basting generously with the lemon-garlic mixture throughout cooking, until blistered on all sides.

Dill Pickles

Servings: 4 | Cooking Time: 10 Minutes

Ingredients:
- 20 dill pickle slices
- ¼ cup all-purpose flour
- ⅛ teaspoon baking powder
- 3 tablespoons beer or seltzer water
- ⅛ teaspoon sea salt
- 2 tablespoons water, plus more if needed
- 2 tablespoons cornstarch
- 1½ cups panko bread crumbs
- 1 teaspoon paprika
- 1 teaspoon garlic powder
- ¼ teaspoon cayenne pepper
- 2 tablespoons canola oil, divided

Directions:
1. Pat the pickle slices dry, and place them on a dry plate in the freezer.
2. In a medium bowl, stir together the flour, baking powder, beer, salt, and water. The batter should be the consistency of cake batter. If it is too thick, add more water, 1 teaspoon at a time.
3. Place the cornstarch in a small shallow bowl.
4. In a separate large shallow bowl, combine the bread crumbs, paprika, garlic powder, and cayenne pepper.
5. Remove the pickles from the freezer. Dredge each one in cornstarch. Tap off any excess, then coat in the batter. Lastly, coat evenly with the bread crumb mixture.
6. Insert the Crisper Basket and close the hood. Select AIR CRISP, set the temperature to 360°F, and set the time to 10 minutes. Select START/STOP to begin preheating.
7. When the unit beeps to signify it has preheated, place the breaded pickles in the basket, stacking them if necessary, and gently brush them with 1 tablespoon of oil. Close the hood and AIR CRISP for 5 minutes.
8. After 5 minutes, shake the basket and gently brush the pickles with the remaining 1 tablespoon of oil. Place the basket back in the unit and close the hood to resume cooking.
9. When cooking is complete, serve immediately.

Jalapeño Poppers

Servings: 4 | Cooking Time: 10 Minutes

Ingredients:
- 8 jalapeños
- 4 ounces cream cheese, at room temperature
- ¼ cup grated Parmesan cheese
- ¼ cup shredded cheddar cheese
- ½ teaspoon garlic powder
- 8 slices thin-cut bacon

Directions:
1. Insert the Grill Grate and close the hood. Select GRILL, set the temperature to HI, and set the time to 10 minutes. Select START/STOP to begin preheating.
2. While the unit is preheating, slice the jalapeños in half lengthwise and scoop out the seeds and membranes.
3. In a small bowl, combine the cream cheese, Parmesan cheese, cheddar cheese, and garlic powder. Scoop the cheese mixture evenly into each jalapeño half.
4. Slice the bacon in half lengthwise so you have 16 strips. Wrap each jalapeño half with a bacon slice, starting from the bottom end and wrapping around until it reaches the top of the jalapeño.
5. When the unit beeps to signify it has preheated, place the jalapeños on the Grill Grate, filling-side up. Close the hood and grill for 10 minutes.
6. When cooking is complete, the bacon will be cooked and beginning to crisp. If you prefer your bacon crispier or charred, continue cooking to your liking. Remove the poppers from the grill and serve.

Twice Air-crisped Potatoes

Servings: 4 | Cooking Time: 40 Minutes

Ingredients:
- 4 medium Idaho or russet potatoes
- Extra-virgin olive oil
- Kosher salt
- 8 tablespoons (1 stick) unsalted butter, at room temperature
- ½ cup sour cream
- 1 cup shredded cheddar cheese
- Freshly ground black pepper

Directions:
1. Insert the Crisper Basket and close the hood. Select AIR CRISP, set the temperature to 400°F, and set the time to 40 minutes. Select START/STOP to begin preheating.
2. While the unit is preheating, rinse and scrub the potatoes. Poke each potato several times with a fork. Brush a generous amount of olive oil over the potatoes and season well with salt.
3. When the unit beeps to signify it has preheated, place the potatoes in the Crisper Basket. Close the hood and cook for 30 minutes.
4. After 30 minutes, open the hood and remove the potatoes. Place on a plate and set aside.
5. Slice the potatoes in half lengthwise. Use a fork to carefully scoop out the insides of the potatoes without damaging the skins. Put the potato flesh in a large bowl. Add the butter, sour cream, and cheddar cheese. Using a spatula, carefully fold the mixture until the butter melts. Scoop the filling into the potato skins. Season each potato half with salt and pepper.
6. Place the loaded potatoes back into the Crisper Basket. Close the hood and cook for 10 minutes more.
7. When cooking is complete, the potato skins will be crispy and the cheese will be melted and infused into the potatoes. Remove the potatoes from the grill and serve.

French Fries

Servings: 4 | Cooking Time: 25 Minutes

Ingredients:
- 1 pound russet or Idaho potatoes, cut in 2-inch strips
- 3 tablespoons canola oil

Directions:
1. Place the potatoes in a large bowl and cover them with cold water. Let soak for 30 minutes. Drain well, then pat with a paper towel until very dry.
2. Insert the Crisper Basket and close the hood. Select AIR CRISP, set the temperature to 390°F, and set the time to 25 minutes. Select START/STOP to begin preheating.
3. Meanwhile, in a large bowl, toss the potatoes with the oil.
4. When the unit beeps to signify it has preheated, add the potatoes to the basket. Close the hood and AIR CRISP for 10 minutes.
5. After 10 minutes, shake the basket well. Place the basket back in the unit and close the hood to resume cooking.
6. After 10 minutes, check for desired crispness. Continue cooking up to 5 minutes more, if necessary.
7. When cooking is complete, serve immediately with your favorite dipping sauce.

Deluxe Cheese Sandwiches

Servings: 4 To 8 | Cooking Time: 5 To 6 Minutes

Ingredients:
- 8 ounces Brie
- 8 slices oat nut bread
- 1 large ripe pear, cored and cut into ½-inch-thick slices
- 2 tablespoons butter, melted

Directions:
1. Select BAKE, set the temperature to 360°F, and set the time to 6 minutes. Select START/STOP to begin preheating. .
2. Make the sandwiches: Spread each of 4 slices of bread with ¼ of the Brie. Top the Brie with the pear slices and remaining 4 bread slices.
3. Brush the melted butter lightly on both sides of each sandwich.
4. Arrange the sandwiches in a baking pan. You may need to work in batches to avoid overcrowding.
5. Place the pan directly in the pot. Close the hood and BAKE for 5 to 6 minutes until the cheese is melted. Repeat with the remaining sandwiches.
6. Serve warm.

Cheesy Garlic Bread

Servings: 4 | Cooking Time: 8 Minutes

Ingredients:
- 1 loaf (about 1 pound) French bread
- 8 tablespoons (1 stick) unsalted butter, at room temperature
- 1 tablespoon minced garlic
- 1 teaspoon garlic powder
- 1½ cups shredded mozzarella cheese
- ½ cup shredded Colby Jack cheese
- 1 teaspoon dried parsley

Directions:
1. Insert the Grill Grate and close the hood. Select GRILL, set the temperature to MED, and set the time to 8 minutes. Select START/STOP to begin preheating.
2. While the unit is preheating, cut the French bread in half lengthwise. In a small bowl, mix together the butter, garlic, and garlic powder until well combined. Spread the garlic butter on both bread halves. Top each half with the mozzarella and Colby Jack cheeses. Sprinkle the dried parsley on top.
3. When the unit beeps to signify it has preheated, place the cheese-topped bread on the Grill Grate. Close the hood and grill for 8 minutes.
4. When cooking is complete, the cheese will be melted and golden brown. Remove the bread from the grill and serve.

Grilled Carrots With Honey Glazed

Servings: 4 | Cooking Time: 10 Minutes

Ingredients:
- 6 medium carrots, peeled and cut lengthwise
- 1 tablespoon canola oil
- 2 tablespoons unsalted butter, melted
- ¼ cup brown sugar, melted
- ¼ cup honey
- ⅛ teaspoon sea salt

Directions:
1. Insert the Grill Grate and close the hood. Select GRILL, set the temperature to MAX, and set the time to 10 minutes. Select START/STOP to begin preheating.
2. In a large bowl, toss the carrots and oil until well coated.
3. When the unit beeps to signify it has preheated, place carrots on the center of the Grill Grate. Close the hood and GRILL for 5 minutes.
4. Meanwhile, in a small bowl, whisk together the butter, brown sugar, honey, and salt.
5. After 5 minutes, open the hood and baste the carrots with the glaze. Using tongs, turn the carrots and baste the other side. Close the hood and GRILL for another 5 minutes.
6. When cooking is complete, serve immediately.

Goat Cheese Bruschetta With Tomatoes

Servings: 4 | Cooking Time: 8 Minutes

Ingredients:
- 8 ounces cherry tomatoes (about 35)
- 8 fresh basil leaves
- 1 tablespoon balsamic vinegar
- 1 (8-ounce) baguette
- ½ cup extra-virgin olive oil
- 2 tablespoons garlic powder
- 8 ounces goat cheese (unflavored)

Directions:
1. Insert the Grill Grate and close the hood. Select GRILL, set the temperature to HI, and set the time to 8 minutes. Select START/STOP to begin preheating.
2. While the unit is preheating, quarter the cherry tomatoes. Slice the basil leaves into very thin ribbons. Place the tomatoes and basil in a medium bowl. Add the balsamic vinegar and toss to coat.
3. Slice the baguette into ½-inch slices. In a small bowl, whisk together the olive oil and garlic powder. Brush both sides of the baguette slices with the olive oil mixture.
4. When the unit beeps to signify it has preheated, place half the baguette slices on the Grill Grate in a single layer. Close the hood and cook for 4 minutes. After 4 minutes, remove the baguettes from the grill and set aside on a plate. Place the remaining slices on the Grill Grate. Close the hood and cook for 4 minutes.
5. When cooking is complete, spread a layer of goat cheese on the baguette slices. Top with the tomato-basil mixture and serve.

Avocado Egg Rolls

Servings: 4 | Cooking Time: 10 Minutes

Ingredients:
- 4 avocados, pitted and diced
- ½ white onion, diced
- ⅓ cup sun-dried tomatoes, chopped
- 1 (16 ounce) package egg roll wrappers (about 20 wrappers)
- ¼ cup water, for sealing
- 4 tablespoons avocado oil

Directions:
1. Insert the Grill Grate and close the hood. Select GRILL, set the temperature to LO, and set the time to 10 minutes. Select START/STOP to begin preheating.
2. While the unit is preheating, place the diced avocado in a large bowl. Add the onion and sun-dried tomatoes and gently fold together, being careful to not mash the avocado.
3. Place an egg roll wrapper on a flat surface with a corner facing you (like a diamond). Add 2 to 3 tablespoons of the filling in the center of the wrapper. The amount should be about 2½ inches wide. Gently lift the bottom corner of the wrapper over the filling, fold in the sides, and roll away from you to close. Dip your finger into the water and run it over the top corner of the wrapper to seal it. Continue filling, folding, and sealing the rest of the egg rolls.
4. When the unit beeps to signify it has preheated, brush the avocado oil on all sides of the egg rolls. Place the egg rolls on the Grill Grate, seam-side down. Close the hood and grill for 5 minutes.
5. After 5 minutes, open the hood and flip the egg rolls. Give them another brush of avocado oil. Close the hood and cook for 5 minutes more.
6. When cooking is complete, the wrappers will be golden brown. Remove from the grill and serve.

Bacon-wrapped Dates

Servings: 6 | Cooking Time: 10 To 14 Minutes

Ingredients:
- 12 dates, pitted
- 6 slices high-quality bacon, cut in half
- Cooking spray

Directions:
1. Insert the Crisper Basket and close the hood. Select BAKE, set the temperature to 360°F, and set the time to 7 minutes. Select START/STOP to begin preheating.
2. Wrap each date with half a bacon slice and secure with a toothpick.
3. Spray the Crisper Basket with cooking spray, then place 6 bacon-wrapped dates in the basket. Place the pan directly in the pot. Close the hood and BAKE for 5 to 7 minutes or until the bacon is crispy. Repeat this process with the remaining dates.
4. Remove the dates and allow to cool on a wire rack for 5 minutes before serving.

Maple Butter Corn Bread

Servings: 4 | Cooking Time: 40 Minutes

Ingredients:
- For the corn bread
- 1 cup all-purpose flour
- 1 cup yellow cornmeal
- 2 teaspoons baking powder
- 1 teaspoon salt
- 1¼ cups milk
- ⅓ cup canola oil
- 1 large egg
- 1 (14.75-ounce) can cream-style sweet corn
- Cooking spray
- For the maple butter
- 1 tablespoon light brown sugar, packed
- 1 tablespoon milk
- 8 tablespoons (1 stick) unsalted butter, at room temperature
- 1 tablespoon maple syrup

Directions:
1. Insert the Cooking Pot and close the hood. Select BAKE, set the temperature to 350°F, and set the time to 40 minutes. Select START/STOP to begin preheating.
2. While the unit is preheating, in a large bowl, combine the flour, cornmeal, baking powder, salt, milk, oil, egg, and sweet corn. Mix until just combined. Grease a 9-by-5-inch loaf pan with cooking spray and pour in the corn bread batter.
3. When the unit beeps to signify it has preheated, place the pan in the Cooking Pot. Close the hood and cook for 40 minutes. If using a metal loaf pan, check the corn bread after 30 minutes, as metal pans may cook faster than glass. Bake until golden brown and the mix is completely baked through.
4. When cooking is complete, the corn bread should be golden brown and a toothpick inserted into the center of the corn bread comes out clean. Remove the pan from the grill and set aside to cool.
5. In a small bowl, whisk together the brown sugar and milk until the sugar is dissolved. Add the butter and continue whisking. Add the maple syrup and continue whisking until fully combined.
6. Cut the corn bread into slices, top with the butter, and serve.

Easy Muffuletta Sliders With Olives

Servings:8 | Cooking Time: 5 To 7 Minutes

Ingredients:

- ¼ pound thinly sliced deli ham
- ¼ pound thinly sliced pastrami
- 4 ounces low-fat Mozzarella cheese, grated
- 8 slider buns, split in half
- Cooking spray
- 1 tablespoon sesame seeds
- Olive Mix:
- ½ cup sliced green olives with pimentos
- ¼ cup sliced black olives
- ¼ cup chopped kalamata olives
- 1 teaspoon red wine vinegar
- ¼ teaspoon basil
- ⅛ teaspoon garlic powder

Directions:

1. Insert the Crisper Basket and close the hood. Select BAKE, set the temperature to 360°F, and set the time to 7 minutes. Select START/STOP to begin preheating.
2. Combine all the ingredients for the olive mix in a small bowl and stir well.
3. Stir together the ham, pastrami, and cheese in a medium bowl and divide the mixture into 8 equal portions.
4. Assemble the sliders: Top each bottom bun with 1 portion of meat and cheese, 2 tablespoons of olive mix, finished by the remaining buns. Lightly spritz the tops with cooking spray. Scatter the sesame seeds on top.
5. Working in batches, arrange the sliders in the Crisper Basket. Close the hood and BAKE for 5 t0 7 minutes until the cheese melts.
6. Transfer to a large plate and repeat with the remaining sliders.
7. Serve immediately.

Queso Bomb

Servings: 6 | Cooking Time: 15 Minutes

Ingredients:

- 1 (1-pound) block easy-melt cheese
- 1 pound ground country breakfast sausage (not links)
- 2 tablespoons minced garlic
- 2 cups shredded Mexican cheese blend or three-cheese blend
- 1 (10-ounce) can diced tomatoes with green chiles
- 1 (10- to 13-ounce) bag tortilla chips

Directions:

1. Insert the Cooking Pot and close the hood. Select GRILL, set the temperature to MED, and set the time to 15 minutes. Select START/STOP to begin preheating.
2. While the unit is preheating, slice the cheese block into 3-inch sections.
3. When the unit beeps to signify it has preheated, place the sausage and garlic in the Cooking Pot. Using a wooden spoon or spatula, break the sausage apart. Close the hood and cook for 5 minutes.
4. After 5 minutes, open the hood and stir the sausage. Add the pieces of easy-melt cheese, then add the shredded cheese blend in an even layer. Pour the diced tomatoes and green chiles with their juices into the pot. Close the hood and cook for 5 minutes.
5. After 5 minutes, stir the sausage and cheese together. Close the hood and cook 5 minutes more.
6. When cooking is complete, the cheese will be fully melted. Serve warm with tortilla chips.

Grilled Shishito Peppers

Servings: 4 | Cooking Time: 10 Minutes

Ingredients:
- 3 cups whole shishito peppers
- 2 tablespoons vegetable oil
- Flaky sea salt, for garnish

Directions:

1. Insert the Grill Grate and close the hood. Select GRILL, set the temperature to MAX, and set the time to 10 minutes. Select START/STOP to begin preheating.

2. While the unit is preheating, in a medium bowl, toss the peppers in the oil until evenly coated.

3. When the unit beeps to signify it has preheated, place the peppers on the Grill Grate. Gently press the peppers down to maximize grill marks. Close the hood and GRILL for 8 to 10 minutes, until they are blistered on all sides.

4. When cooking is complete, place the peppers in a serving dish and top with the flaky sea salt. Serve immediately.

Rosemary Baked Cashews

Servings:2 | Cooking Time: 3 Minutes

Ingredients:
- 2 sprigs of fresh rosemary
- 1 teaspoon olive oil
- 1 teaspoon kosher salt
- ½ teaspoon honey
- 2 cups roasted and unsalted whole cashews
- Cooking spray

Directions:

1. Insert the Crisper Basket and close the hood. Select BAKE, set the temperature to 300°F, and set the time to 3 minutes. Select START/STOP to begin preheating.

2. In a medium bowl, whisk together the chopped rosemary, olive oil, kosher salt, and honey. Set aside.

3. Spray the Crisper Basket with cooking spray, then place the cashews and the whole rosemary sprig in the basket. Close the hood and BAKE for 3 minutes.

4. Remove the cashews and rosemary from the grill, then discard the rosemary and add the cashews to the olive oil mixture, tossing to coat.

5. Allow to cool for 15 minutes before serving.

Sweet Potato Chips

Servings:1 | Cooking Time: 8 To 10 Hours

Ingredients:
- 1 sweet potato, peeled
- ½ tablespoon avocado oil
- ½ teaspoon sea salt

Directions:
1. Using a mandoline, thinly slice (⅛ inch or less) the sweet potato.
2. In a large bowl, toss the sweet potato slices with the oil until evenly coated. Season with the salt.
3. Place the sweet potato slices flat on the Crisper Basket. Arrange them in a single layer, without any slices touching each another.
4. Place the basket in the pot and close the hood.
5. Select DEHYDRATE, set the temperature to 120ºF, and set the time to 10 hours. Select START/STOP.
6. After 8 hours, check for desired doneness. Continue dehydrating for 2 more hours, if necessary.
7. When cooking is complete, remove the basket from the pot. Transfer the sweet potato chips to an airtight container and store at room temperature.

Zucchini And Potato Tots

Servings: 4 | Cooking Time: 20 Minutes

Ingredients:
- 1 large zucchini, grated
- 1 medium baked potato, skin removed and mashed
- ¼ cup shredded Cheddar cheese
- 1 large egg, beaten
- ½ teaspoon kosher salt
- Cooking spray

Directions:
1. Select AIR CRISP, set the temperature to 390ºF, and set the time to 10 minutes. Select START/STOP to begin preheating.
2. Wrap the grated zucchini in a paper towel and squeeze out any excess liquid, then combine the zucchini, baked potato, shredded Cheddar cheese, egg, and kosher salt in a large bowl.
3. Spray a baking pan with cooking spray, then place individual tablespoons of the zucchini mixture in the pan. Place the pan directly in the pot. Close the hood and AIR CRISP for 10 minutes. Repeat this process with the remaining mixture.
4. Remove the tots and allow to cool on a wire rack for 5 minutes before serving.

Cheesy Summer Squash With Red Onion

Servings: 4 | Cooking Time: 15 Minutes

Ingredients:
- ½ cup vegetable oil, plus 3 tablespoons
- ¼ cup white wine vinegar
- 1 garlic clove, grated
- 2 summer squash, sliced lengthwise about ¼-inch thick
- 1 red onion, peeled and cut into wedges
- Sea salt, to taste
- Freshly ground black pepper, to taste
- 1 package crumbled feta cheese
- Red pepper flakes, as needed

Directions:
1. Insert the Grill Grate and close the hood. Select GRILL, set the temperature to MAX, and set the time to 15 minutes. Select START/STOP to begin preheating.
2. Meanwhile, in a small bowl, whisk together ½ cup oil, vinegar, and garlic, and set aside.
3. In a large bowl, toss the squash and onion with remaining 3 tablespoons of oil until evenly coated. Season with the salt and pepper.
4. When the unit beeps to signify it has preheated, arrange the squash and onions on the Grill Grate. Close the hood and GRILL for 6 minutes.
5. After 6 minutes, open the hood and flip the squash. Close the hood and GRILL for 6 to 9 minutes more.
6. When vegetables are cooked to desired doneness, remove them from the grill. Arrange the vegetables on a large platter and top with the feta cheese. Drizzle the dressing over the top, and sprinkle with the red pepper flakes. Let stand for 15 minutes before serving.

Blt With Grilled Heirloom Tomato

Servings: 4 | Cooking Time: 10 Minutes

Ingredients:
- 8 slices white bread
- 8 tablespoons mayonnaise
- 2 heirloom tomatoes, sliced ¼-inch thick
- 2 tablespoons canola oil
- Sea salt, to taste
- Freshly ground black pepper, to taste
- 8 slices bacon, cooked
- 8 leaves iceberg lettuce

Directions:
1. Insert the Grill Grate, and close the hood. Select GRILL, set the temperature to MAX, and set the time to 10 minutes. Select START/STOP to begin preheating.
2. While the unit is preheating, spread a thin layer of mayonnaise on one side of each piece of bread.
3. When the unit beeps to signify it has preheated, place the bread, mayonnaise-side down, on the Grill Grate. Close the hood and GRILL for 2 to 3 minutes, until crisp.
4. Meanwhile, remove the watery pulp and seeds from the tomato slices. Brush both sides of the tomatoes with the oil and season with salt and pepper.
5. After 2 to 3 minutes, remove the bread and place the tomatoes on the grill. Close the hood and continue grilling for the remaining 6 to 8 minutes.
6. To assemble, spread a thin layer of mayonnaise on the non-grilled sides of the bread. Layer the tomatoes, bacon, and lettuce on the bread, and top with the remaining slices of bread. Slice each sandwich in half and serve.

Servings: 4 | Cooking Time: 15 Minutes

Ingredients:
- 8 ounces cream cheese, at room temperature
- 1 (13-ounce) can marinated artichoke quarters, drained and coarsely chopped
- ½ cup sour cream
- ½ cup grated Parmesan cheese
- ¼ teaspoon garlic powder
- 2 cups shredded mozzarella
- 1 (6-ounce) package mini pita bread rounds
- Extra-virgin olive oil
- Chopped fresh chives, for garnish

Directions:

1. Insert the Cooking Pot and close the hood. Select GRILL, set the temperature to MED, and set the time to 15 minutes. Select START/STOP to begin preheating.

2. While the unit is preheating, place the cream cheese, artichokes, sour cream, Parmesan cheese, garlic powder, and mozzarella cheese in a 9-by-5-inch loaf pan. Stir until well combined.

3. When the unit beeps to signify it has preheated, place the pan in the Cooking Pot. Close the hood and cook for 5 minutes.

4. After 5 minutes, open the hood and stir the dip with a wooden spoon, holding onto the loaf pan with grill mitts. Close the hood and cook for 7 minutes more.

5. Meanwhile, place the Grill Grate next to the Foodi™ Grill. Put the pita rounds in a large bowl and drizzle with the olive oil. Toss to coat. Place the pita rounds on the Grill Grate.

6. After 7 minutes, open the hood. Remove the pan of artichoke dip from the Cooking Pot. Place the Grill Grate into the unit. Close the hood and cook for the remaining 3 minutes.

7. Cooking is complete when the pita chips are warm and crispy. Garnish the dip with the fresh chives and serve.

POULTRY

Turkey Jerky

Servings: 2 | Cooking Time: 3 To 5 Hours

Ingredients:

- 1 pound turkey breast, very thinly sliced
- 1 cup soy sauce
- 2 tablespoons light brown sugar, packed
- 2 tablespoons Worcestershire sauce
- ½ teaspoon garlic powder
- ½ teaspoon onion powder
- ½ teaspoon red pepper flakes

Directions:

1. In a resealable bag, combine the turkey, soy sauce, brown sugar, Worcestershire sauce, garlic powder, onion powder, and red pepper flakes. Massage the turkey slices so all are fully coated in the marinade. Seal the bag and refrigerate overnight.
2. An hour before you plan to put the turkey in the dehydrator, remove the turkey slices from the marinade and place them between two paper towels to dry out and come to room temperature.
3. Once dried, lay the turkey slices flat in the Crisper Basket in a single layer. Insert the Crisper Basket in the Cooking Pot and close the hood. Select DEHYDRATE, set the temperature to 150°F, and set the time to 5 hours. Select START/STOP.
4. After 3 hours, check for desired doneness. Continue dehydrating for up to 2 more hours, if desired.
5. When cooking is complete, the jerky should have a dry texture. Remove from the basket and serve, or store in a resealable bag in the refrigerator for up to 2 weeks.

Pecan-crusted Turkey Cutlets

Servings: 4 | Cooking Time: 10 To 12 Minutes

Ingredients:

- ¾ cup panko bread crumbs
- ¼ teaspoon salt
- ¼ teaspoon pepper
- ¼ teaspoon dry mustard
- ¼ teaspoon poultry seasoning
- ½ cup pecans
- ¼ cup cornstarch
- 1 egg, beaten
- 1 pound turkey cutlets, ½-inch thick
- Salt and pepper, to taste
- Cooking spray

Directions:

1. Insert the Crisper Basket and close the hood. Select AIR CRISP, set the temperature to 360°F, and set the time to 12 minutes. Select START/STOP to begin preheating.
2. Place the panko crumbs, salt, pepper, mustard, and poultry seasoning in a food processor. Process until crumbs are finely crushed. Add pecans and process just until nuts are finely chopped.
3. Place cornstarch in a shallow dish and beaten egg in another. Transfer coating mixture from food processor into a third shallow dish.
4. Sprinkle turkey cutlets with salt and pepper to taste.
5. Dip cutlets in cornstarch and shake off excess, then dip in beaten egg and finally roll in crumbs, pressing to coat well. Spray both sides with cooking spray.
6. Place 2 cutlets in Crisper Basket in a single layer. Close the hood and AIR CRISP for 10 to 12 minutes. Repeat with the remaining cutlets.
7. Serve warm.

Lime-garlic Grilled Chicken

Servings: 4 | Cooking Time: 18 Minutes

Ingredients:
- 1½ tablespoons extra-virgin olive oil
- 3 garlic cloves, minced
- ¼ teaspoon ground cumin
- Sea salt, to taste
- Freshly ground black pepper, to taste
- Grated zest of 1 lime
- Juice of 1 lime
- 4 boneless, skinless chicken breasts

Directions:

1. In a large shallow bowl, stir together the oil, garlic, cumin, salt, pepper, zest, and lime juice. Add the chicken breasts and coat well. Cover and marinate in the refrigerator for 30 minutes.

2. Insert the Grill Grate and close the hood. Select GRILL, set the temperature to MEDIUM, and set the time to 18 minutes. Select START/STOP to begin preheating.

3. When the unit has beeped to signify it has preheated, place the chicken breasts on the Grill Grate. Close the hood and GRILL for 7 minutes. After 7 minutes, flip the chicken, close the hood, and GRILL for an additional 7 minutes.

4. Check the chicken for doneness. If needed, GRILL up to 4 minutes more. Cooking is complete when the internal temperature of the chicken reaches at least 165°F on a food thermometer.

5. Remove from the grill, and place on a cutting board or platter to rest for 5inutes. Serve.

Sriracha-honey Glazed Chicken Thighs

Servings: 4 | Cooking Time: 17 Minutes

Ingredients:
- 1 cup sriracha
- Juice of 2 lemons
- ¼ cup honey
- 4 bone-in chicken thighs

Directions:

1. Place the sriracha, lemon juice, and honey in a large resealable plastic bag or container. Add the chicken thighs and toss to coat evenly. Refrigerate for 30 minutes.

2. Insert the Grill Grate and close the hood. Select GRILL, set the temperature to MEDIUM, and set the time to 14 minutes. Select START/STOP to begin preheating.

3. When the unit beeps to signify it has preheated, place the chicken thighs onto the Grill Grate, gently pressing them down to maximize grill marks. Close the hood and GRILL for 7 minutes.

4. After 7 minutes, flip the chicken thighs using tongs. Close the hood and GRILL for 7 minutes more.

5. Cooking is complete when the internal temperature of the meat reaches at least 165°F on a food thermometer. If necessary, close the hood and continue grilling for 2 to 3 minutes more.

6. When cooking is complete, remove the chicken from the grill, and let it rest for 5 minutes before serving.

Servings: 4 | Cooking Time: 14 Minutes

Ingredients:
- 1 cup maple syrup
- ⅓ cup soy sauce
- ¼ cup teriyaki sauce
- 3 garlic cloves, minced
- 2 teaspoons garlic powder
- 2 teaspoons onion powder
- 1 teaspoon freshly ground black pepper
- 2 pounds bone-in chicken wings (drumettes and flats)

Directions:

1. Insert the Grill Grate and close the hood. Select GRILL, set the temperature to MEDIUM, and set the time to 14 minutes. Select START/STOP to begin preheating.
2. Meanwhile, in a large bowl, whisk together the maple syrup, soy sauce, teriyaki sauce, garlic, garlic powder, onion powder, and black pepper. Add the wings, and use tongs to toss and coat.
3. When the unit has beeped to signify it has preheated, place the chicken wings on the Grill Grate. Close the hood and GRILL for 5 minutes. After 5 minutes, flip the wings, close the hood, and GRILL for an additional 5 minutes.
4. Check the wings for doneness. Cooking is complete when the internal temperature of the meat reaches at least 165°F on a food thermometer. If needed, GRILL for up to 4 minutes more.
5. Remove from the grill and serve.

Teriyaki Chicken And Bell Pepper Kebabs

Servings: 4 | Cooking Time: 14 Minutes

Ingredients:
- 1 pound boneless, skinless chicken breasts, cut into 2-inch cubes
- 1 cup teriyaki sauce, divided
- 2 green bell peppers, seeded and cut into 1-inch cubes
- 2 cups fresh pineapple, cut into 1-inch cubes

Directions:

1. Place the chicken and ½ cup of teriyaki sauce in a large resealable plastic bag or container. Toss to coat evenly. Refrigerate for at least 30 minutes.
2. Insert the Grill Grate and close the hood. Select GRILL, set the temperature to MEDIUM, and set the time to 14 minutes. Select START/STOP to begin preheating.
3. While the unit is preheating, assemble the kebabs by threading the chicken onto the wood skewers, alternating with the peppers and pineapple. Ensure the ingredients are pushed almost completely down to the end of the skewers.
4. When the unit beeps to signify it has preheated, place the skewers on the Grill Grate. Close the hood and GRILL for 10 to 14 minutes, occasionally basting the kebabs with the remaining ½ cup of teriyaki sauce while cooking.
5. Cooking is complete when the internal temperature of the chicken reaches 165°F on a food thermometer.

Lemon And Rosemary Chicken

Servings: 4 | Cooking Time: 15 Minutes

Ingredients:
- 3 pounds bone-in, skin-on chicken thighs
- 4 tablespoons avocado oil
- 2 tablespoons lemon-pepper seasoning
- 1 tablespoon chopped fresh rosemary
- 1 lemon, thinly sliced

Directions:
1. Insert the Grill Grate and close the hood. Select GRILL, set the temperature to LO, and set the time to 15 minutes. Select START/STOP to begin preheating.
2. Coat the chicken thighs with the avocado oil and rub the lemon-pepper seasoning and rosemary evenly over the chicken.
3. When the unit beeps to signify it has preheated, place the chicken thighs on the Grill Grate, skin-side up. Place the lemon slices on top of the chicken. Close the hood and grill for 8 minutes.
4. After 8 minutes, open the hood and remove the lemon slices. Flip the chicken and place the lemon slices back on top. Close the hood and cook for 7 minutes more.
5. When cooking is complete, remove the chicken from the grill and serve.

Potato Cheese Crusted Chicken

Servings: 4 | Cooking Time: 22 To 25 Minutes

Ingredients:
- ¼ cup buttermilk
- 1 large egg, beaten
- 1 cup instant potato flakes
- ¼ cup grated Parmesan cheese
- 1 teaspoon salt
- ½ teaspoon freshly ground black pepper
- 2 whole boneless, skinless chicken breasts, halved
- Cooking spray

Directions:
1. Insert the Crisper Basket and close the hood. Select BAKE, set the temperature to 325°F, and set the time to 25 minutes. Select START/STOP to begin preheating.
2. Line the Crisper Basket with parchment paper.
3. In a shallow bowl, whisk the buttermilk and egg until blended. In another shallow bowl, stir together the potato flakes, cheese, salt, and pepper.
4. One at a time, dip the chicken pieces in the buttermilk mixture and the potato flake mixture, coating thoroughly.
5. Place the coated chicken on the parchment and spritz with cooking spray.
6. Close the hood and BAKE for 15 minutes. Flip the chicken, spritz it with cooking spray, and bake for 7 to 10 minutes more until the outside is crispy and the inside is no longer pink. Serve immediately.

Adobo Chicken

Servings: 4 | Cooking Time: 15 Minutes

Ingredients:

- 2 tablespoons soy sauce
- 2 tablespoons rice vinegar
- 1 tablespoon balsamic vinegar
- ¼ teaspoon freshly ground black pepper
- 4 garlic cloves, minced
- ½ teaspoon peeled minced fresh ginger
- Juice of ½ lemon
- ¼ teaspoon granulated sugar
- 3 bay leaves
- Pinch Italian seasoning (optional)
- Pinch ground cumin (optional)
- 3 pounds chicken drumsticks

Directions:

1. In a large bowl, whisk together the soy sauce, rice vinegar, balsamic vinegar, pepper, garlic, ginger, lemon juice, sugar, bay leaves, Italian seasoning (if using), and cumin (if using). Add the drumsticks to the marinade, making sure the meat is coated. Cover and refrigerate for at least 1 hour. If you have the time, marinate the chicken overnight to let all the flavors settle in.
2. Insert the Grill Grate and close the hood. Select GRILL, set the temperature to MED, and set the time to 15 minutes. Select START/STOP to begin preheating.
3. When the unit beeps to signify it has preheated, place the chicken drumsticks on the Grill Grate. Brush any leftover marinade onto the drumsticks. Close the hood and grill for 8 minutes.
4. After 8 minutes, open the hood and flip the drumsticks. Close the hood and continue cooking for 7 minutes more.
5. When cooking is complete, remove the drumsticks from the grill and serve.

Sweet Chili Turkey Kebabs

Servings: 4 | Cooking Time: 12 Minutes

Ingredients:

- 2 pounds turkey breast, cut into 1-inch cubes
- ¼ cup honey
- 1 tablespoon extra-virgin olive oil
- 2 tablespoons apple cider vinegar
- 2 tablespoons soy sauce
- Juice of 1 lime
- 1 teaspoon red pepper flakes

Directions:

1. Place 5 or 6 turkey cubes on each of 8 to 10 skewers. In a zip-top bag, combine the honey, olive oil, vinegar, soy sauce, lime juice, and red pepper flakes. Shake to mix well. Place the turkey skewers in the marinade and massage to coat the meat. Seal the bag and let marinate at room temperature for 30 minutes or in the refrigerator overnight.
2. Insert the Grill Grate and close the hood. Select GRILL, set the temperature to MED, and set the time to 12 minutes. Select START/STOP to begin preheating.
3. When the unit beeps to signify it has preheated, place half of the skewers on the Grill Grate. Brush extra glaze on the skewers. Close the hood and grill for 3 minutes.
4. After 3 minutes, open the hood and flip the skewers. Close the hood and cook for 3 minutes more.
5. After 3 minutes, remove the skewers from the grill. Repeat steps 3 and 4 for the remaining skewers.
6. When cooking is complete, remove the kebabs from the grill and serve.

Spicy Bbq Chicken Drumsticks

Servings: 4 | Cooking Time: 20 Minutes

Ingredients:
- 2 cups barbecue sauce
- Juice of 1 lime
- 2 tablespoons honey
- 1 tablespoon hot sauce
- Sea salt, to taste
- Freshly ground black pepper, to taste
- 1 pound chicken drumsticks

Directions:

1. In a large bowl, combine the barbecue sauce, lime juice, honey, and hot sauce. Season with salt and pepper. Set aside ½ cup of the sauce. Add the drumsticks to the bowl, and toss until evenly coated.

2. Insert the Grill Grate and close the hood. Select GRILL, set the temperature to MEDIUM, and set the time to 20 minutes. Select START/STOP to begin preheating.

3. When the unit beeps to signify it has preheated, place the drumsticks on the Grill Grate. Close the hood and GRILL for 18 minutes, basting often during cooking.

4. Cooking is complete when the internal temperature of the meat reaches at least 165°F on a food thermometer. If necessary, close the hood and continue grilling for 2 minutes more.

Blackened Chicken

Servings: 4 | Cooking Time: 10 Minutes

Ingredients:
- 1 tablespoon paprika
- 1 tablespoon garlic powder
- 1 tablespoon onion powder
- 1 tablespoon freshly ground black pepper
- 1 teaspoon Italian seasoning
- 1 teaspoon salt
- ½ teaspoon ground cumin
- ½ teaspoon cayenne pepper
- 4 tablespoons (½ stick) unsalted butter, melted
- ¼ cup avocado oil
- 4 boneless, skinless chicken breasts (about 2 pounds), halved crosswise

Directions:

1. Insert the Grill Grate and close the hood. Select GRILL, set the temperature to HI, and set the time to 10 minutes. Select START/STOP to begin preheating.

2. In a small bowl, combine the paprika, garlic powder, onion powder, black pepper, Italian seasoning, salt, cumin, and cayenne pepper.

3. In a separate small bowl, whisk together the butter and avocado oil. Lightly coat the chicken breasts on both sides with the butter-and-oil mixture, and then season both sides with the spice mix to get a nice coating.

4. When the unit beeps to signify it has preheated, open the hood and place the seasoned chicken on the Grill Grate. Close the hood and grill for 5 minutes.

5. After 5 minutes, open the hood and flip the chicken. Close the hood and cook for 5 minutes more.

6. When cooking is complete, remove the chicken from the grill and serve.

Sweet-and-sour Drumsticks

Servings: 4 | Cooking Time: 23 To 25 Minutes

Ingredients:
- 6 chicken drumsticks
- 3 tablespoons lemon juice, divided
- 3 tablespoons low-sodium soy sauce, divided
- 1 tablespoon peanut oil
- 3 tablespoons honey
- 3 tablespoons brown sugar
- 2 tablespoons ketchup
- ¼ cup pineapple juice

Directions:
1. Insert the Crisper Basket and close the hood. Select BAKE, set the temperature to 350°F, and set the time to 18 minutes. Select START/STOP to begin preheating.
2. Sprinkle the drumsticks with 1 tablespoon of lemon juice and 1 tablespoon of soy sauce. Place in the Crisper Basket and drizzle with the peanut oil. Toss to coat. Close the hood and BAKE for 18 minutes, or until the chicken is almost done.
3. Meanwhile, in a metal bowl, combine the remaining 2 tablespoons of lemon juice, the remaining 2 tablespoons of soy sauce, honey, brown sugar, ketchup, and pineapple juice.
4. Add the cooked chicken to the bowl and stir to coat the chicken well with the sauce.
5. Place the metal bowl in the basket. Bake for 5 to 7 minutes or until the chicken is glazed and registers 165°F on a meat thermometer. Serve warm.

Spiced Breaded Chicken Cutlets

Servings: 2 | Cooking Time: 11 Minutes

Ingredients:
- ½ pound boneless, skinless chicken breasts, horizontally sliced in half, into cutlets
- ½ tablespoon extra-virgin olive oil
- ⅛ cup bread crumbs
- ¼ teaspoon sea salt
- ¼ teaspoon freshly ground black pepper
- ¼ teaspoon paprika
- ¼ teaspoon garlic powder
- ⅛ teaspoon onion powder

Directions:
1. Insert the Crisper Basket and close the hood. Select AIR CRISP, set the temperature to 375°F, and set the time to 11 minutes. Select START/STOP to begin preheating.
2. Brush each side of the chicken cutlets with the oil.
3. Combine the bread crumbs, salt, pepper, paprika, garlic powder, and onion powder in a medium shallow bowl. Dredge the chicken cutlets in the bread crumb mixture, turning several times, to ensure the chicken is fully coated.
4. When the unit beeps to signify it has preheated, place the chicken in the basket. Close the hood and AIR CRISP for 9 minutes. Cooking is complete when the internal temperature of the meat reaches at least 165°F on a food thermometer. If needed, AIR CRISP for up to 2 minutes more.
5. Remove the chicken cutlets and serve immediately.

Servings: 6 | Cooking Time: 15 Minutes

Ingredients:
- 1 pound lean ground turkey
- ½ cup whole-wheat panko bread crumbs
- 1 egg, beaten
- 1 tablespoon soy sauce
- ¼ cup plus 1 tablespoon hoisin sauce, divided
- 2 teaspoons minced garlic
- ⅛ teaspoon salt
- ⅛ teaspoon freshly ground black pepper
- 1 teaspoon sriracha
- Olive oil spray

Directions:
1. Spray the Crisper Basket lightly with olive oil spray.
2. Insert the Crisper Basket and close the hood. Select AIR CRISP, set the temperature to 350°F, and set the time to 15 minutes. Select START/STOP to begin preheating.
3. In a large bowl, mix together the turkey, panko bread crumbs, egg, soy sauce, 1 tablespoon of hoisin sauce, garlic, salt, and black pepper.
4. Using a tablespoon, form the mixture into 24 meatballs.
5. In a small bowl, combine the remaining ¼ cup of hoisin sauce and sriracha to make a glaze and set aside.
6. Place the meatballs in the Crisper Basket in a single layer. You may need to cook them in batches.
7. Close the hood and AIR CRISP for 8 minutes. Brush the meatballs generously with the glaze and AIR CRISP until cooked through, an additional 4 to 7 minutes.
8. Serve warm.

Honey Rosemary Chicken

Servings: 4 | Cooking Time: 20 Minutes

Ingredients:
- ¼ cup balsamic vinegar
- ¼ cup honey
- 2 tablespoons olive oil
- 1 tablespoon dried rosemary leaves
- 1 teaspoon salt
- ½ teaspoon freshly ground black pepper
- 2 whole boneless, skinless chicken breasts, halved
- Cooking spray

Directions:
1. In a large resealable bag, combine the vinegar, honey, olive oil, rosemary, salt, and pepper. Add the chicken pieces, seal the bag, and refrigerate to marinate for at least 2 hours.
2. Insert the Crisper Basket and close the hood. Select BAKE, set the temperature to 325°F, and set the time to 20 minutes. Select START/STOP to begin preheating.
3. Line the Crisper Basket with parchment paper.
4. Remove the chicken from the marinade and place it on the parchment. Spritz with cooking spray.
5. Close the hood and BAKE for 10 minutes. Flip the chicken, spritz it with cooking spray, and bake for 10 minutes more until the internal temperature reaches 165°F and the chicken is no longer pink inside. Let sit for 5 minutes before serving.

Mini Turkey Meatloaves With Carrot

Servings: 4 | Cooking Time: 20 To 24 Minutes

Ingredients:
- ⅓ cup minced onion
- ¼ cup grated carrot
- 2 garlic cloves, minced
- 2 tablespoons ground almonds
- 2 teaspoons olive oil
- 1 teaspoon dried marjoram
- 1 egg white
- ¾ pound ground turkey breast

Directions:
1. Select BAKE, set the temperature to 400ºF, and set the time to 24 minutes. Select START/STOP to begin pre-heating.
2. In a medium bowl, stir together the onion, carrot, garlic, almonds, olive oil, marjoram, and egg white.
3. Add the ground turkey. With your hands, gently but thoroughly mix until combined.
4. Double 16 foil muffin cup liners to make 8 cups. Divide the turkey mixture evenly among the liners. Transfer to the pot.
5. Close the hood and BAKE for 20 to 24 minutes, or until the meatloaves reach an internal temperature of 165ºF on a meat thermometer. Serve immediately.

Roasted Cajun Turkey

Servings: 4 | Cooking Time: 30 Minutes

Ingredients:
- 2 pounds turkey thighs, skinless and boneless
- 1 red onion, sliced
- 2 bell peppers, sliced
- 1 habanero pepper, minced
- 1 carrot, sliced
- 1 tablespoon Cajun seasoning mix
- 1 tablespoon fish sauce
- 2 cups chicken broth
- Nonstick cooking spray

Directions:
1. Select ROAST, set the temperature to 360ºF, and set the time to 30 minutes. Select START/STOP to begin preheating.
2. Spritz the bottom and sides of the pot with nonstick cooking spray.
3. Arrange the turkey thighs in the pot. Add the onion, peppers, and carrot. Sprinkle with Cajun seasoning. Add the fish sauce and chicken broth.
4. Close the hood and ROAST for 30 minutes until cooked through. Serve warm.

Ginger Chicken Thighs

Servings: 4 | Cooking Time: 10 Minutes

Ingredients:
- ¼ cup julienned peeled fresh ginger
- 2 tablespoons vegetable oil
- 1 tablespoon honey
- 1 tablespoon soy sauce
- 1 tablespoon ketchup
- 1 teaspoon garam masala
- 1 teaspoon ground turmeric
- ¼ teaspoon kosher salt
- ½ teaspoon cayenne pepper
- Vegetable oil spray
- 1 pound boneless, skinless chicken thighs, cut crosswise into thirds
- ¼ cup chopped fresh cilantro, for garnish

Directions:

1. In a small bowl, combine the ginger, oil, honey, soy sauce, ketchup, garam masala, turmeric, salt, and cayenne. Whisk until well combined. Place the chicken in a resealable plastic bag and pour the marinade over. Seal the bag and massage to cover all of the chicken with the marinade. Marinate at room temperature for 30 minutes or in the refrigerator for up to 24 hours.

2. Insert the Crisper Basket and close the hood. Select BAKE, set the temperature to 350ºF, and set the time to 10 minutes. Select START/STOP to begin preheating.

3. Spray the Crisper Basket with vegetable oil spray and add the chicken and as much of the marinade and julienned ginger as possible.

4. Close the hood and BAKE for 10 minutes. Use a meat thermometer to ensure the chicken has reached an internal temperature of 165ºF.

5. To serve, garnish with cilantro.

Strawberry-glazed Turkey

Servings: 2 | Cooking Time: 37 Minutes

Ingredients:
- 2 pounds turkey breast
- 1 tablespoon olive oil
- Salt and ground black pepper, to taste
- 1 cup fresh strawberries

Directions:

1. Insert the Crisper Basket and close the hood. Select AIR CRISP, set the temperature to 375ºF, and set the time to 37 minutes. Select START/STOP to begin preheating.

2. Rub the turkey bread with olive oil on a clean work surface, then sprinkle with salt and ground black pepper.

3. Transfer the turkey in the basket. Close the hood and AIR CRISP for 30 minutes or until the internal temperature of the turkey reaches at least 165ºF. flip the turkey breast halfway through.

4. Meanwhile, put the strawberries in a food processor and pulse until smooth.

5. When the cooking of the turkey is complete, spread the puréed strawberries over the turkey. Close the hood and AIR CRISP for 7 more minutes.

6. Serve immediately.

Servings: 4 | Cooking Time: 20 Minutes

Ingredients:

- 1 tablespoon olive oil
- 1 pound boneless, skinless chicken tenderloins
- 1 teaspoon salt
- ½ teaspoon freshly ground black pepper
- ½ teaspoon paprika
- ½ teaspoon garlic powder
- ½ cup whole-wheat seasoned bread crumbs
- 1 teaspoon dried parsley
- Cooking spray

Directions:

1. Spray the Crisper Basket lightly with cooking spray.

2. Insert the Crisper Basket and close the hood. Select AIR CRISP, set the temperature to 370°F, and set the time to 20 minutes. Select START/STOP to begin preheating.

3. In a medium bowl, toss the chicken with the salt, pepper, paprika, and garlic powder until evenly coated.

4. Add the olive oil and toss to coat the chicken evenly.

5. In a separate, shallow bowl, mix together the bread crumbs and parsley.

6. Coat each piece of chicken evenly in the bread crumb mixture.

7. Place the chicken in the Crisper Basket in a single layer and spray it lightly with cooking spray. You may need to cook them in batches.

8. Close the hood and AIR CRISP for 10 minutes. Flip the chicken over, lightly spray it with cooking spray, and AIR CRISP for an additional 8 to 10 minutes, until golden brown. Serve.

MEATLESS

Grilled Artichokes With Garlic Aioli

Servings: 4 | Cooking Time: 33 Minutes

Ingredients:
- For the artichokes
- 4 artichokes
- 8 tablespoons avocado oil
- 8 tablespoons minced garlic
- Salt
- Freshly ground black pepper
- For the garlic aioli
- ½ cup mayonnaise
- 1 garlic clove, minced
- 1 tablespoon apple cider vinegar
- ⅛ teaspoon paprika

Directions:
1. Pull off the tough outer leaves near the stem of the artichoke and trim the bottom of the stem. Cut off the top third (½ to 1 inch) of the artichoke. Trim the tips of the leaves that surround the artichoke, as they can be sharp and thorny. Then cut the artichoke in half lengthwise. This exposes the artichoke heart. Use a spoon to remove the fuzzy choke, scraping to make sure it is cleaned away, then rinse the artichoke.
2. Insert the Grill Grate and close the hood. Select GRILL, set the temperature to LO, and set the time to 25 minutes. Select START/STOP to begin preheating.
3. While the unit is preheating, prepare 8 large pieces of aluminum foil for wrapping. Place an artichoke half, cut-side up, in the center of a foil piece. Drizzle 1 tablespoon of avocado oil into the center of the artichoke half and add 1 tablespoon of minced garlic. Season with salt and pepper. Seal the foil packet, making sure all sides are closed. Repeat for each artichoke half.
4. When the unit beeps to signify it has preheated, place the foil-wrapped artichokes on the Grill Grate. Close the hood and grill for 25 minutes.
5. When cooking is complete, the stem and heart will be soft, about the consistency of a cooked potato. Remove the artichokes from the foil.
6. Select GRILL, set the temperature to MAX, and set the time to 8 minutes. Place the artichokes on the Grill Grate, cut-side down. Select START/STOP and then press the PREHEAT button to skip preheating. Close the hood and cook for 4 minutes.
7. After 4 minutes, open the hood and flip the artichokes. Season with additional salt and pepper, if desired. Close the hood and cook for 4 minutes more.
8. When cooking is complete, remove the artichokes from the grill.
9. In a small bowl, combine the mayonnaise, garlic, vinegar, and paprika. Serve alongside the artichokes for dipping.

Kidney Beans Oatmeal In Peppers

Servings: 2 To 4 | Cooking Time: 6 Minutes

Ingredients:
- 2 large bell peppers, halved lengthwise, deseeded
- 2 tablespoons cooked kidney beans
- 2 tablespoons cooked chick peas
- 2 cups cooked oatmeal
- 1 teaspoon ground cumin
- ½ teaspoon paprika
- ½ teaspoon salt or to taste
- ¼ teaspoon black pepper powder
- ¼ cup yogurt

Directions:
1. Insert the Crisper Basket and close the hood. Select AIR CRISP, set the temperature to 355ºF, and set the time to 6 minutes. Select START/STOP to begin preheating.
2. Put the bell peppers, cut-side down, in the Crisper Basket. Close the hood and AIR CRISP for 2 minutes.
3. Take the peppers out of the grill and let cool.
4. In a bowl, combine the rest of the ingredients.
5. Divide the mixture evenly and use each portion to stuff a pepper.
6. Return the stuffed peppers to the basket. Close the hood and AIR CRISP for 4 minutes.
7. Serve hot.

Garlic Roasted Asparagus

Servings: 4 | Cooking Time: 10 Minutes

Ingredients:
- 1 pound asparagus, woody ends trimmed
- 2 tablespoons olive oil
- 1 tablespoon balsamic vinegar
- 2 teaspoons minced garlic
- Salt and freshly ground black pepper, to taste

Directions:
1. Insert the Crisper Basket and close the hood. Select ROAST, set the temperature to 400ºF, and set the time to 10 minutes. Select START/STOP to begin preheating.
2. In a large shallow bowl, toss the asparagus with the olive oil, balsamic vinegar, garlic, salt, and pepper until thoroughly coated.
3. Arrange the asparagus in the Crisper Basket. Close the hood and ROAST for 10 minutes until crispy. Flip the asparagus with tongs halfway through the cooking time.
4. Serve warm.

Beef Stuffed Bell Peppers

Servings: 4 | Cooking Time: 30 Minutes

Ingredients:
- 1 pound ground beef
- 1 tablespoon taco seasoning mix
- 1 can diced tomatoes and green chilis
- 4 green bell peppers
- 1 cup shredded Monterey jack cheese, divided

Directions:
1. Insert the Crisper Basket and close the hood. Select AIR CRISP, set the temperature to 350°F, and set the time to 15 minutes. Select START/STOP to begin preheating.
2. Set a skillet over a high heat and cook the ground beef for 8 minutes. Make sure it is cooked through and browned all over. Drain the fat.
3. Stir in the taco seasoning mix, and the diced tomatoes and green chilis. Allow the mixture to cook for a further 4 minutes.
4. In the meantime, slice the tops off the green peppers and remove the seeds and membranes.
5. When the meat mixture is fully cooked, spoon equal amounts of it into the peppers and top with the Monterey jack cheese. Then place the peppers into the basket. Close the hood and AIR CRISP for 15 minutes.
6. The peppers are ready when they are soft, and the cheese is bubbling and brown. Serve warm.

Simple Ratatouille

Servings: 2 | Cooking Time: 16 Minutes

Ingredients:
- 2 Roma tomatoes, thinly sliced
- 1 zucchini, thinly sliced
- 2 yellow bell peppers, sliced
- 2 garlic cloves, minced
- 2 tablespoons olive oil
- 2 tablespoons herbes de Provence
- 1 tablespoon vinegar
- Salt and black pepper, to taste

Directions:
1. Select ROAST, set the temperature to 390°F, and set the time to 16 minutes. Select START/STOP to begin preheating.
2. Place the tomatoes, zucchini, bell peppers, garlic, olive oil, herbes de Provence, and vinegar in a large bowl and toss until the vegetables are evenly coated. Sprinkle with salt and pepper and toss again. Pour the vegetable mixture into the pot.
3. Close the hood and ROAST for 8 minutes. Stir and continue roasting for 8 minutes until tender.
4. Let the vegetable mixture stand for 5 minutes in the basket before removing and serving.

Perfect Grilled Asparagus

Servings: 4 | Cooking Time: 6 Minutes

Ingredients:
- 24 asparagus spears, woody ends trimmed
- Extra-virgin olive oil, for drizzling
- Sea salt
- Freshly ground black pepper

Directions:
1. Insert the Grill Grate and close the hood. Select GRILL, set the temperature to HI, and set the time to 6 minutes. Select START/STOP to begin preheating.
2. While the unit is preheating, place the asparagus in a large bowl and drizzle with the olive oil. Toss to coat, then season with salt and pepper.
3. When the unit beeps to signify it has preheated, place the spears evenly spread out on the Grill Grate. Close the hood and grill for 3 minutes.
4. After 3 minutes, open the hood and flip and move the spears around. Close the hood and cook for 3 minutes more.
5. When cooking is complete, remove the asparagus from the grill and serve.

Honey-glazed Baby Carrots

Servings: 4 | Cooking Time: 12 Minutes

Ingredients:
- 1 pound baby carrots
- 2 tablespoons olive oil
- 1 tablespoon honey
- 1 teaspoon dried dill
- Salt and black pepper, to taste

Directions:
1. Insert the Crisper Basket and close the hood. Select ROAST, set the temperature to 350ºF, and set the time to 12 minutes. Select START/STOP to begin preheating.
2. Place the carrots in a large bowl. Add the olive oil, honey, dill, salt, and pepper and toss to coat well.
3. Arrange the carrots in the Crisper Basket. Close the hood and ROAST for 12 minutes, until crisp-tender. Shake the basket once during cooking.
4. Serve warm.

Cinnamon-spiced Acorn Squash

Servings: 2 | Cooking Time: 15 Minutes

Ingredients:
- 1 medium acorn squash, halved crosswise and de-seeded
- 1 teaspoon coconut oil
- 1 teaspoon light brown sugar
- Few dashes of ground cinnamon
- Few dashes of ground nutmeg

Directions:
1. Insert the Crisper Basket and close the hood. Select AIR CRISP, set the temperature to 325ºF, and set the time to 15 minutes. Select START/STOP to begin preheating.
2. On a clean work surface, rub the cut sides of the acorn squash with coconut oil. Scatter with the brown sugar, cinnamon, and nutmeg.
3. Put the squash halves in the Crisper Basket, cut-side up. Close the hood and AIR CRISP for 15 minutes until just tender when pierced in the center with a paring knife.
4. Rest for 5 to 10 minutes and serve warm.

Balsamic Mushroom Sliders With Pesto

Servings: 4 | Cooking Time: 8 Minutes

Ingredients:
- 8 small portobello mushrooms, trimmed with gills removed
- 2 tablespoons canola oil
- 2 tablespoons balsamic vinegar
- 8 slider buns
- 1 tomato, sliced
- ½ cup pesto
- ½ cup micro greens

Directions:
1. Insert the Grill Grate and close the hood. Select GRILL, set the temperature to HIGH, and set the time to 8 minutes. Select START/STOP to begin preheating.
2. While the unit is preheating, brush the mushrooms with the oil and balsamic vinegar.
3. When the unit beeps to signify it has preheated, place the mushrooms, gill-side down, on the Grill Grate. Close the hood and GRILL for 8 minutes until the mushrooms are tender.
4. When cooking is complete, remove the mushrooms from the grill, and layer on the buns with tomato, pesto, and micro greens.

Charred Green Beans With Sesame Seeds

Servings: 4 | Cooking Time: 8 Minutes

Ingredients:
- 1 tablespoon reduced-sodium soy sauce or tamari
- ½ tablespoon Sriracha sauce
- 4 teaspoons toasted sesame oil, divided
- 12 ounces trimmed green beans
- ½ tablespoon toasted sesame seeds

Directions:
1. Insert the Crisper Basket and close the hood. Select AIR CRISP, set the temperature to 375°F, and set the time to 8 minutes. Select START/STOP to begin preheating.
2. Whisk together the soy sauce, Sriracha sauce, and 1 teaspoon of sesame oil in a small bowl until smooth.
3. Toss the green beans with the remaining sesame oil in a large bowl until evenly coated.
4. Place the green beans in the Crisper Basket in a single layer. You may need to work in batches to avoid over-crowding.
5. Close the hood and AIR CRISP for 8 minutes until the green beans are lightly charred and tender. Shake the basket halfway through the cooking time.
6. Remove from the basket to a platter. Repeat with the remaining green beans.
7. Pour the prepared sauce over the top of green beans and toss well. Serve sprinkled with the toasted sesame seeds.

Servings: 4 | Cooking Time: 25 Minutes

Ingredients:
- Chermoula:
- 1 cup packed fresh cilantro leaves
- ½ cup packed fresh parsley leaves
- 6 cloves garlic, peeled
- 2 teaspoons smoked paprika
- 2 teaspoons ground cumin
- 1 teaspoon ground coriander
- ½ to 1 teaspoon cayenne pepper
- Pinch of crushed saffron (optional)
- ½ cup extra-virgin olive oil
- Kosher salt, to taste
- Beets:
- 3 medium beets, trimmed, peeled, and cut into 1-inch chunks
- 2 tablespoons chopped fresh cilantro
- 2 tablespoons chopped fresh parsley

Directions:
1. In a food processor, combine the cilantro, parsley, garlic, paprika, cumin, coriander, and cayenne. Pulse until coarsely chopped. Add the saffron, if using, and process until combined. With the food processor running, slowly add the olive oil in a steady stream; process until the sauce is uniform. Season with salt.
2. Insert the Crisper Basket and close the hood. Select ROAST, set the temperature to 375ºF, and set the time to 25 minutes. Select START/STOP to begin preheating.
3. In a large bowl, drizzle the beets with ½ cup of the chermoula to coat. Arrange the beets in the Crisper Basket. Close the hood and ROAST for 25 minutes, or until the beets are tender.
4. Transfer the beets to a serving platter. Sprinkle with the chopped cilantro and parsley and serve.

Servings: 4 | Cooking Time: 15 Minutes

Ingredients:
- Vegetable oil spray
- 1 package frozen spinach, thawed and squeezed dry
- ½ cup chopped onion
- 2 cloves garlic, minced
- 4 ounces cream cheese, diced
- ½ teaspoon ground nutmeg
- 1 teaspoon kosher salt
- 1 teaspoon black pepper
- ½ cup grated Parmesan cheese

Directions:
1. Select BAKE, set the temperature to 350ºF, and set the time to 15 minutes. Select START/STOP to begin preheating.
2. Spray a heatproof pan with vegetable oil spray.
3. In a medium bowl, combine the spinach, onion, garlic, cream cheese, nutmeg, salt, and pepper. Transfer to the prepared pan.
4. Place the pan directly in the pot. Close the hood and BAKE for 10 minutes. Open and stir to thoroughly combine the cream cheese and spinach.
5. Sprinkle the Parmesan cheese on top. Bake for 5 minutes, or until the cheese has melted and browned.
6. Serve hot.

Servings:3 | Cooking Time: 20 Minutes

Ingredients:
- Glaze:
- 2 tablespoons raw honey
- 2 teaspoons minced garlic
- ¼ teaspoon dried marjoram
- ¼ teaspoon dried basil
- ¼ teaspoon dried oregano
- ⅛ teaspoon dried sage
- ⅛ teaspoon dried rosemary
- ⅛ teaspoon dried thyme
- ½ teaspoon salt
- ¼ teaspoon ground black pepper
- Veggies:
- 3 to 4 medium red potatoes, cut into 1- to 2-inch pieces
- 1 small zucchini, cut into 1- to 2-inch pieces
- 1 small carrot, sliced into ¼-inch rounds
- 1 package cherry tomatoes, halved
- 1 cup sliced mushrooms
- 3 tablespoons olive oil

Directions:
1. Insert the Crisper Basket and close the hood. Select ROAST, set the temperature to 380ºF, and set the time to 15 minutes. Select START/STOP to begin preheating.
2. Combine the honey, garlic, marjoram, basil, oregano, sage, rosemary, thyme, salt, and pepper in a small bowl and stir to mix well. Set aside.
3. Place the red potatoes, zucchini, carrot, cherry tomatoes, and mushroom in a large bowl. Drizzle with the olive oil and toss to coat.
4. Pour the veggies into the Crisper Basket. Close the hood and ROAST for 15 minutes, shaking the basket halfway through.
5. When ready, transfer the roasted veggies to the large bowl. Pour the honey mixture over the veggies, tossing to coat.
6. Spread out the veggies in a baking pan and place in the grill.
7. Increase the temperature to 390ºF and ROAST for an additional 5 minutes, or until the veggies are tender and glazed. Serve warm.

Roasted Butternut Squash

Servings: 6 To 8

Cooking Time: 40 Minutes

Ingredients:
- 2 butternut squash
- Avocado oil, for drizzling
- Salt
- Freshly ground black pepper

Directions:
1. Cut off the stem end of each squash, then cut the squash in half lengthwise. To do this, carefully rock the knife back and forth to cut through the tough skin and flesh. Use a spoon to scrape out the seeds from each half.
2. Insert the Cooking Pot and close the hood. Select ROAST, set the temperature to 400°F, and set the time to 40 minutes. Select START/STOP to begin preheating.
3. While the unit is preheating, drizzle the avocado oil over the butternut squash flesh. I also like to rub it in with my hands. Season with salt and pepper.
4. When the unit beeps to signify it has preheated, place the butternut squash in the Cooking Pot, cut-side down. Close the hood and cook for 40 minutes.
5. When cooking is complete, the flesh will be soft and easy to scoop out with a spoon. Remove from the grill and serve.

Cheesy Macaroni Balls

Servings: 2 | Cooking Time: 10 Minutes

Ingredients:
- 2 cups leftover macaroni
- 1 cup shredded Cheddar cheese
- ½ cup flour
- 1 cup bread crumbs
- 3 large eggs
- 1 cup milk
- ½ teaspoon salt
- ¼ teaspoon black pepper

Directions:

1. Insert the Crisper Basket and close the hood. Select AIR CRISP, set the temperature to 365°F, and set the time to 10 minutes. Select START/STOP to begin preheating.
2. In a bowl, combine the leftover macaroni and shredded cheese.
3. Pour the flour in a separate bowl. Put the bread crumbs in a third bowl. Finally, in a fourth bowl, mix the eggs and milk with a whisk.
4. With an ice-cream scoop, create balls from the macaroni mixture. Coat them the flour, then in the egg mixture, and lastly in the bread crumbs.
5. Arrange the balls in the basket. Close the hood and AIR CRISP for 10 minutes, giving them an occasional stir. Ensure they crisp up nicely.
6. Serve hot.

Rosemary Roasted Squash With Cheese

Servings: 2 | Cooking Time: 20 Minutes

Ingredients:
- 1 pound butternut squash, cut into wedges
- 2 tablespoons olive oil
- 1 tablespoon dried rosemary
- Salt, to salt
- 1 cup crumbled goat cheese
- 1 tablespoon maple syrup

Directions:

1. Insert the Crisper Basket and close the hood. Select ROAST, set the temperature to 350°F, and set the time to 20 minutes. Select START/STOP to begin preheating.
2. Toss the squash wedges with the olive oil, rosemary, and salt in a large bowl until well coated.
3. Transfer the squash wedges to the Crisper Basket, spreading them out in as even a layer as possible.
4. Close the hood and ROAST for 10 minutes. Flip the squash and roast for another 10 minutes until golden brown.
5. Sprinkle the goat cheese on top and serve drizzled with the maple syrup.

Simple Pesto Gnocchi

Servings: 4 | Cooking Time: 15 Minutes

Ingredients:
- 1 package gnocchi
- 1 medium onion, chopped
- 3 cloves garlic, minced
- 1 tablespoon extra-virgin olive oil
- 1 jar pesto
- ⅓ cup grated Parmesan cheese

Directions:
1. Insert the Crisper Basket and close the hood. Select AIR CRISP, set the temperature to 340ºF, and set the time to 15 minutes. Select START/STOP to begin preheating.
2. In a large bowl combine the onion, garlic, and gnocchi, and drizzle with the olive oil. Mix thoroughly.
3. Transfer the mixture to the basket. Close the hood and AIR CRISP for 15 minutes, stirring occasionally, making sure the gnocchi become light brown and crispy.
4. Add the pesto and Parmesan cheese, and give everything a good stir before serving.

Cheesy Rice And Olives Stuffed Peppers

Servings: 4 | Cooking Time: 16 To 17 Minutes

Ingredients:
- 4 red bell peppers, tops sliced off
- 2 cups cooked rice
- 1 cup crumbled feta cheese
- 1 onion, chopped
- ¼ cup sliced kalamata olives
- ¾ cup tomato sauce
- 1 tablespoon Greek seasoning
- Salt and black pepper, to taste
- 2 tablespoons chopped fresh dill, for serving

Directions:
1. Select BAKE, set the temperature to 360ºF, and set the time to 15 minutes. Select START/STOP to begin preheating.
2. Microwave the red bell peppers for 1 to 2 minutes until tender.
3. When ready, transfer the red bell peppers to a plate to cool.
4. Mix together the cooked rice, feta cheese, onion, kalamata olives, tomato sauce, Greek seasoning, salt, and pepper in a medium bowl and stir until well combined.
5. Divide the rice mixture among the red bell peppers and transfer to a greased baking pan.
6. Place the pan directly in the pot. Close the hood and BAKE for 15 minutes, or until the rice is heated through and the vegetables are soft.
7. Remove from the basket and serve with the dill sprinkled on top.

Prosciutto Mini Mushroom Pizza

Servings: 3 | Cooking Time: 5 Minutes

Ingredients:
- 3 portobello mushroom caps, cleaned and scooped
- 3 tablespoons olive oil
- Pinch of salt
- Pinch of dried Italian seasonings
- 3 tablespoons tomato sauce
- 3 tablespoons shredded Mozzarella cheese
- 12 slices prosciutto

Directions:
1. Insert the Crisper Basket and close the hood. Select AIR CRISP, set the temperature to 330ºF, and set the time to 5 minutes. Select START/STOP to begin preheating.
2. Season both sides of the portobello mushrooms with a drizzle of olive oil, then sprinkle salt and the Italian seasonings on the insides.
3. With a knife, spread the tomato sauce evenly over the mushroom, before adding the Mozzarella on top.
4. Put the portobello in the Crisper Basket. Close the hood and AIR CRISP for 1 minutes, before taking the Crisper Basket out of the grill and putting the prosciutto slices on top. AIR CRISP for another 4 minutes.
5. Serve warm.

Stuffed Squash With Tomatoes And Poblano

Servings: 4 | Cooking Time: 30 Minutes

Ingredients:
- 1 pound butternut squash, ends trimmed
- 2 teaspoons olive oil, divided
- 6 grape tomatoes, halved
- 1 poblano pepper, cut into strips
- Salt and black pepper, to taste
- ¼ cup grated Mozzarella cheese

Directions:
1. Insert the Crisper Basket and close the hood. Select ROAST, set the temperature to 350ºF, and set the time to 30 minutes. Select START/STOP to begin preheating.
2. Using a large knife, cut the squash in half lengthwise on a flat work surface. This recipe just needs half of the squash. Scoop out the flesh to make room for the stuffing. Coat the squash half with 1 teaspoon of olive oil.
3. Put the squash half in the Crisper Basket. Close the hood and ROAST for 15 minutes.
4. Meanwhile, thoroughly combine the tomatoes, poblano pepper, remaining 1 teaspoon of olive oil, salt, and pepper in a bowl.
5. Remove the basket and spoon the tomato mixture into the squash. Return to the grill and roast for 12 minutes until the tomatoes are soft.
6. Scatter the Mozzarella cheese on top and continue roasting for about 3 minutes, or until the cheese is melted.
7. Cool for 5 minutes before serving.

Servings: 4 | Cooking Time: 15 Minutes

Ingredients:
- 1 (15-ounce) can pinto beans, drained and rinsed
- 1 tablespoon chili powder
- 2 teaspoons ground cumin
- 2 teaspoons sea salt
- 1 teaspoon paprika
- ½ teaspoon garlic powder
- ½ teaspoon onion powder
- ½ teaspoon dried oregano
- 4 small flour tortillas
- 1 cup sour cream
- 1 (14-ounce) can diced tomatoes, drained
- 1 (15-ounce) can black beans, drained and rinsed
- 2 cups shredded cheddar cheese

Directions:
1. Insert the Cooking Pot and close the hood. Select BAKE, set the temperature to 350°F, and set the time to 15 minutes. Select START/STOP to begin preheating.
2. While the unit is preheating, in a large bowl, mash the pinto beans with a fork. Add the chili powder, cumin, salt, paprika, garlic powder, onion powder, and oregano and mix until well combined. Place a tortilla in the bottom of a 6-inch springform pan. Spread a quarter of the mashed pinto beans on the tortilla in an even layer, then layer on a quarter each of the sour cream, tomatoes, black beans, and cheddar cheese in that order. Repeat the layers three more times, ending with cheese.
3. When the unit beeps to signify it has preheated, place the pan in the Cooking Pot. Close the hood and cook for 15 minutes.
4. When cooking is complete, the cheese will be melted. Remove the pan from the grill and serve.

MEATS

Cheesy Jalapeño Popper Burgers

Servings: 4 | Cooking Time: 9 Minutes

Ingredients:

- 2 jalapeño peppers, seeded, stemmed, and minced
- ½ cup shredded Cheddar cheese
- 4 ounces cream cheese, at room temperature
- 4 slices bacon, cooked and crumbled
- 2 pounds ground beef
- ½ teaspoon chili powder
- ¼ teaspoon paprika
- ¼ teaspoon freshly ground black pepper
- 4 hamburger buns
- 4 slices pepper Jack cheese
- Lettuce, sliced tomato, and sliced red onion, for topping (optional)

Directions:

1. Insert the Grill Grate and close the hood. Select GRILL, set the temperature to HIGH, and set the time to 9 minutes. Select START/STOP to begin preheating.
2. In a medium bowl, combine the peppers, Cheddar cheese, cream cheese, and bacon until well combined.
3. Form the ground beef into 8¼-inch-thick patties. Spoon some of the filling mixture onto four of the patties, then place a second patty on top of each to make four burgers. Use your fingers to pinch the edges of the patties together to seal in the filling. Reshape the patties with your hands as needed.
4. Combine the chili powder, paprika, and pepper in a small bowl. Sprinkle the mixture onto both sides of the burgers.
5. When the units beeps to signify it has preheated, place the burgers on the Grill Grate. Close the hood and GRILL for 4 minutes without flipping. Cooking is complete when the internal temperature of the beef reaches at least 145ºF on a food thermometer. If needed, GRILL for up to 5 more minutes.
6. Place the burgers on the hamburger buns and top with pepper Jack cheese. Add lettuce, tomato, and red onion, if desired.

Spaghetti Squash Lasagna

Servings: 6 | Cooking Time: 1 Hour 15 Minutes

Ingredients:

- 2 large spaghetti squash, cooked
- 4 pounds ground beef
- 1 large jar Marinara sauce
- 25 slices Mozzarella cheese
- 30 ounces whole-milk ricotta cheese

Directions:

1. Select BAKE, set the temperature to 375ºF, and set the time to 45 minutes. Select START/STOP to begin pre-heating.
2. Slice the spaghetti squash and place it face down inside a baking pan. Fill with water until covered.
3. Place the pan directly in the pot. Close the hood and BAKE for 45 minutes until skin is soft.
4. Sear the ground beef in a skillet over medium-high heat for 5 minutes or until browned, then add the marinara sauce and heat until warm. Set aside.
5. Scrape the flesh off the cooked squash to resemble strands of spaghetti.
6. Layer the lasagna in a large greased pan in alternating layers of spaghetti squash, beef sauce, Mozzarella, ricotta. Repeat until all the ingredients have been used.
7. Place the pan directly in the pot. Close the hood and BAKE for 30 minutes.
8. Serve.

Green Curry Beef

Servings: 4 | Cooking Time: 12 Minutes

Ingredients:
- 1 yellow onion
- 1 red bell pepper
- 2 pounds sirloin steak
- 1 tablespoon minced garlic
- 1 tablespoon light brown sugar, packed
- 2 tablespoons green curry paste
- 1 teaspoon salt
- ½ teaspoon freshly ground black pepper
- Juice of ½ lime
- 1 (13-ounce) can full-fat unsweetened coconut milk
- 2 tablespoons fish sauce (optional)
- 1 cup fresh Thai basil or sweet basil

Directions:

1. Insert the Cooking Pot and close the hood. Select GRILL, set the temperature to MED, and set the time to 12 minutes. Select START/STOP to begin preheating.

2. While the unit is preheating, dice the onion, slice the red bell pepper, and thinly slice the steak into bite-size strips.

3. When the unit beeps to signify it has preheated, place the onion and garlic in the Cooking Pot. Then add the beef and stir with a wooden spoon. Close the hood and cook for 4 minutes.

4. After 4 minutes, open the hood and add the brown sugar, green curry paste, salt, pepper, lime juice, coconut milk, and fish sauce (if using). Close the hood and cook for 4 minutes. After 4 minutes, open the hood and stir the curry. Close the hood and cook for 4 minutes more.

5. When cooking is complete, open the hood, add the basil, and stir one more time. Close the hood and let the coconut curry sit for 5 minutes before serving.

Lemongrass Beef Skewers

Servings: 4 | Cooking Time: 8 Minutes

Ingredients:
- 3 tablespoons minced garlic
- 3 tablespoons light brown sugar, packed
- 3 tablespoons lemongrass paste
- 1 tablespoon soy sauce
- 1 tablespoon peeled minced fresh ginger
- 1 tablespoon avocado oil
- ½ small red onion, minced
- 2 pounds sirloin steak, cut into 1-inch cubes
- Chopped fresh cilantro, for garnish

Directions:

1. In a large bowl, combine the garlic, brown sugar, lemongrass paste, soy sauce, ginger, avocado oil, and onion until the sugar is dissolved. Add the steak cubes and massage them with the marinade. Place 5 or 6 cubes on each of 6 to 8 skewers, then place the skewers in a large rimmed baking sheet and coat with the remaining marinade. Set aside to marinate for at least 30 minutes. If marinating for longer, cover and refrigerate.

2. Insert the Grill Grate and close the hood. Select GRILL, set the temperature to HI, and set the time to 8 minutes. Select START/STOP to begin preheating.

3. When the unit beeps to signify it has preheated, place the skewers on the Grill Grate. Close the hood and grill for 4 minutes.

4. After 4 minutes, open the hood and flip the skewers. Close the hood and cook for 4 minutes more. If you prefer extra char, add 2 minutes to the cook time.

5. When cooking is complete, remove the skewers from the grill and serve, garnished with the cilantro.

Spicy Pork Chops With Carrots And Mushrooms

Servings: 4 | Cooking Time: 15 To 18 Minutes

Ingredients:

- 2 carrots, cut into sticks
- 1 cup mushrooms, sliced
- 2 garlic cloves, minced
- 2 tablespoons olive oil
- 1 pound boneless pork chops
- 1 teaspoon dried oregano
- 1 teaspoon dried thyme
- 1 teaspoon cayenne pepper
- Salt and ground black pepper, to taste
- Cooking spray

Directions:

1. Spritz the Crisper Basket with cooking spray.
2. Insert the Crisper Basket and close the hood. Select AIR CRISP, set the temperature to 360°F, and set the time to 18 minutes. Select START/STOP to begin preheating.
3. In a mixing bowl, toss together the carrots, mushrooms, garlic, olive oil and salt until well combined.
4. Add the pork chops to a different bowl and season with oregano, thyme, cayenne pepper, salt and black pepper.
5. Lower the vegetable mixture in the prepared Crisper Basket. Place the seasoned pork chops on top. Close the hood and AIR CRISP for 15 to 18 minutes, or until the pork is well browned and the vegetables are tender, flipping the pork and shaking the basket once halfway through.
6. Transfer the pork chops to the serving dishes and let cool for 5 minutes. Serve warm with vegetable on the side.

Honey-garlic Ribs

Servings: 6 | Cooking Time: 1 Hour 10 Minutes

Ingredients:

- 2 (2- to 3-pound) racks baby back ribs
- Sea salt
- ½ cup soy sauce
- 1 cup honey
- 4 garlic cloves, minced
- 1 teaspoon paprika
- 3 tablespoons light brown sugar, packed

Directions:

1. Insert the Grill Grate and close the hood. Select BAKE, set the temperature to 300°F, and set the time to 1 hour. Select START/STOP to begin preheating.
2. While the unit is preheating, generously season each rack with salt, then wrap each in aluminum foil.
3. When the unit beeps to signify it has preheated, place the foil-wrapped ribs on the Grill Grate. Close the hood and cook for 1 hour.
4. While the ribs are cooking, in a small bowl, combine the soy sauce, honey, garlic, paprika, and brown sugar until the sugar is dissolved.
5. When cooking is complete, remove the ribs from the grill. Slowly open the foil (but don't remove it) and brush the sauce over the ribs. Pour the remaining sauce over both racks.
6. Place the slightly opened packets of racks back onto the Grill Grate. Select GRILL, set the temperature to HI, and set the time to 10 minutes. Select START/STOP and then press the PREHEAT button to skip preheating. Close the hood and cook for 5 minutes.
7. After 5 minutes, open the hood, flip the rib racks, and place them back in the foil. Close the hood and cook for 5 minutes more or until you achieve your desired level of char.
8. When cooking is complete, remove the racks from the grill and serve.

Potato And Prosciutto Salad

Servings: 8 | Cooking Time: 7 Minutes

Ingredients:
- Salad:
- 4 pounds potatoes, boiled and cubed
- 15 slices prosciutto, diced
- 2 cups shredded Cheddar cheese
- Dressing:
- 15 ounces sour cream
- 2 tablespoons mayonnaise
- 1 teaspoon salt
- 1 teaspoon black pepper
- 1 teaspoon dried basil

Directions:
1. Select AIR CRISP, set the temperature to 350°F, and set the time to 7 minutes. Select START/STOP to begin preheating.
2. Put the potatoes, prosciutto, and Cheddar in a baking pan. Place the pan directly in the pot. Close the hood and AIR CRISP for 7 minutes.
3. In a separate bowl, mix the sour cream, mayonnaise, salt, pepper, and basil using a whisk.
4. Coat the salad with the dressing and serve.

Rack Of Lamb Chops With Rosemary

Servings: 2 | Cooking Time: 14 Minutes

Ingredients:
- 3 tablespoons extra-virgin olive oil
- 1 garlic clove, minced
- 1 tablespoon fresh rosemary, chopped
- ½ rack lamb
- Sea salt, to taste
- Freshly ground black pepper, to taste

Directions:
1. Combine the oil, garlic, and rosemary in a large bowl. Season the rack of lamb with the salt and pepper, then place the lamb in the bowl, using tongs to turn and coat fully in the oil mixture. Cover and refrigerate for 2 hours.
2. Insert the Grill Grate and close the hood. Select GRILL, set the temperature to HIGH, and set the time to 14 minutes. Select START/STOP to begin preheating.
3. When the unit beeps to signify it has preheated, place the lamb on the Grill Grate. Close the hood and GRILL for 6 minutes. After 6 minutes, flip the lamb and continue grilling for 6 minutes more.
4. Cooking is complete when the internal temperature of the lamb reaches 145°F on a food thermometer. If needed, GRILL for up to 2 minutes more.

Balsamic Honey Mustard Lamb Chops

Servings: 4 To 6 | Cooking Time: 45 Minutes To 1 Hour

Ingredients:

- ¼ cup avocado oil
- ½ cup balsamic vinegar
- 2 garlic cloves, minced
- 1 teaspoon salt
- ½ teaspoon freshly ground black pepper
- 2 tablespoons honey
- 1 tablespoon yellow mustard
- 1 tablespoon fresh rosemary
- 1 (2- to 3-pound) rack of lamb

Directions:

1. In a large bowl, whisk together the avocado oil, vinegar, garlic, salt, pepper, honey, mustard, and rosemary. Add the lamb and massage and coat all sides of the meat with the marinade. Cover and refrigerate for at least 1 hour.
2. Plug the thermometer into the unit. Insert the Cooking Pot and close the hood. Select ROAST, set the temperature to 350°F, and select PRESET. Use the arrows to the right to select BEEF/ LAMB. The unit will default to WELL to cook lamb to a safe temperature. Insert the Smart Thermometer in the thickest part of the lamb without touching bone. Select START/STOP to begin preheating.
3. When the unit beeps to signify it has preheated, place the rack of lamb in the Cooking Pot. Close the hood to begin cooking.
4. When cooking is complete, the Smart Thermometer will indicate that the specified internal temperature has been reached. Remove the lamb from the pot and serve.

Beef And Scallion Rolls

Servings: 4 | Cooking Time: 10 Minutes

Ingredients:

- 1 pound skirt steak, very thinly sliced (12 slices)
- Salt
- Freshly ground black pepper
- 6 scallions, both white and green parts, halved lengthwise
- 2 tablespoons cornstarch
- ¼ cup water
- ¼ cup soy sauce
- 2 tablespoons light brown sugar, packed
- 1 teaspoon peeled minced fresh ginger
- 1 teaspoon garlic powder

Directions:

1. Insert the Grill Grate and close the hood. Select GRILL, set the temperature to HI, and set the time to 10 minutes. Select START/STOP to begin preheating.
2. While the unit is preheating, season each steak slice with salt and pepper. With one of the longer sides of a steak slice closest to you, place a scallion length at the bottom, and roll away from you to wrap the scallion. Sprinkle cornstarch on the outer layer of the rolled-up steak. Repeat for the remaining steak slices, scallions, and cornstarch.
3. In a small bowl, mix together the water, soy sauce, brown sugar, ginger, and garlic until the sugar is dissolved.
4. When the unit beeps to signify it has preheated, dip each beef roll in the soy sauce mixture and place it on the Grill Grate, seam-side down. Close the hood and grill for 5 minutes.
5. After 5 minutes, open the hood and flip the beef rolls. Brush each roll with the marinade. Close the hood and cook for 5 minutes more.
6. When cooking is complete, remove the beef rolls from the grill and serve.

Servings: 8 | Cooking Time: 15 Minutes

Ingredients:

- 1 (4-pound) boneless center-cut pork loin
- ½ cup avocado oil
- ½ cup grated Parmesan cheese
- 2 tablespoons finely chopped fresh basil
- 1 tablespoon finely chopped fresh parsley
- 1 tablespoon chopped fresh chives
- ½ teaspoon finely chopped fresh rosemary
- 5 garlic cloves, minced

Directions:

1. Butterfly the pork loin. You can use the same method as you would for a chicken breast or steak (see here), but because a pork loin is thicker, you can perform this double butterfly technique: Place the boneless, trimmed loin on a cutting board. One-third from the bottom of the loin, slice horizontally from the side (parallel to the cutting board), stopping about ½ inch from the opposite side, and open the flap like a book. Make another horizontal cut from the thicker side of the loin to match the thickness of the first cut, stopping again ½ inch from the edge. Open up the flap to create a rectangular piece of flat meat.

2. Plug the thermometer into the unit. Insert the Grill Grate and close the hood. Select GRILL, set the temperature to MED, and select PRESET. Use the arrows to the right to select PORK. The unit will default to WELL to cook pork to a safe temperature. Select START/STOP to begin preheating.

3. While the unit is preheating, in a small bowl, combine the avocado oil, Parmesan cheese, basil, parsley, chives, rosemary, and garlic. Spread the pesto sauce evenly over the cut side of each tenderloin. Starting from a longer side, roll up the pork tightly over the filling. Use toothpicks to secure the ends. Insert the Smart Thermometer into the thickest part of the meat.

4. When the unit beeps to signify it has preheated, place the loin on the Grill Grate. Close the hood to begin cooking.

5. When the Foodi™ Grill indicates it's time to flip, open the hood and flip the loin. Close the hood to continue cooking.

6. When cooking is complete, the Smart Thermometer will indicate that the internal temperature has been reached. Open the hood and remove the loin. Let the meat rest for 10 minutes before slicing in between the toothpicks. Serve.

Grilled Pork Banh Mi

Servings: 6 | Cooking Time: 15 Minutes

Ingredients:

- 3 tablespoons light brown sugar, packed
- 1 tablespoon soy sauce
- 3 tablespoons minced garlic
- Juice of 2 limes
- 1 shallot, finely minced
- 2 pounds pork tenderloin, cut into 1-inch-thick slices
- 1 daikon radish, cut into thin strips
- 1 large carrot, cut into thin strips
- 3 tablespoons rice vinegar
- ½ teaspoon kosher salt
- 1 teaspoon granulated sugar
- 6 sandwich-size baguettes
- Mayonnaise
- 1 cucumber, thinly sliced
- Fresh cilantro
- 1 jalapeño, sliced

Directions:

1. In a large bowl, combine the brown sugar, soy sauce, garlic, lime juice, shallot, and pork tenderloin slices. Marinate for at least 30 minutes. If marinating for longer, cover and refrigerate.
2. Insert the Cooking Pot and close the hood. Select GRILL, set the temperature to HI, and set the time to 15 minutes. Select START/STOP to begin preheating.
3. While the unit is preheating, in a medium bowl, combine the daikon, carrot, rice vinegar, salt, and sugar.
4. When the unit beeps to signify it has preheated, place the pork in the Cooking Pot. Feel free to add a little bit of the marinade to the pot. Close the hood and cook for 8 minutes.
5. After 8 minutes, open the hood and stir the pork. Close the hood and cook for 7 minutes more.
6. When cooking is complete, slice open each baguette and spread mayonnaise on both sides. Add a layer each of pork, pickled daikon and carrot, cucumber, cilantro, and jalapeño slices and serve.

Baby Back Ribs In Gochujang Marinade

Servings: 4 | Cooking Time: 22 Minutes

Ingredients:

- ¼ cup gochujang paste
- ¼ cup soy sauce
- ¼ cup freshly squeezed orange juice
- 2 tablespoons apple cider vinegar
- 2 tablespoons sesame oil
- 6 garlic cloves, minced
- 1½ tablespoons brown sugar
- 1 tablespoon grated fresh ginger
- 1 teaspoon salt
- 4 baby back ribs

Directions:

1. In a medium bowl, add the gochujang paste, soy sauce, orange juice, vinegar, oil, garlic, sugar, ginger, and salt, and stir to combine.
2. Place the baby back ribs on a baking sheet and coat all sides with the sauce. Cover with aluminum foil and refrigerate for 6 hours.
3. Insert the Grill Grate and close the hood. Select GRILL, set the temperature to MEDIUM, and set the time to 22 minutes. Select START/STOP to begin preheating.
4. When the unit beeps to signify it has preheated, place the ribs on the Grill Grate. Close the hood and GRILL for 11 minutes. After 11 minutes, flip the ribs, close the hood, and GRILL for an additional 11 minutes.
5. When cooking is complete, serve immediately.

Miso Marinated Steak

Servings: 4 | Cooking Time: 12 Minutes

Ingredients:
- ¾ pound flank steak
- 1½ tablespoons sake
- 1 tablespoon brown miso paste
- 1 teaspoon honey
- 2 cloves garlic, pressed
- 1 tablespoon olive oil

Directions:
1. Put all the ingredients in a Ziploc bag. Shake to cover the steak well with the seasonings and refrigerate for at least 1 hour.
2. Insert the Crisper Basket and close the hood. Select AIR CRISP, set the temperature to 400°F, and set the time to 12 minutes. Select START/STOP to begin preheating.
3. Coat all sides of the steak with cooking spray. Put the steak in the basket.
4. Close the hood and AIR CRISP for 12 minutes, turning the steak twice during the cooking time, then serve immediately.

Garlic Herb Crusted Lamb

Servings: 6 | Cooking Time: 1 Hour

Ingredients:
- ¼ cup red wine vinegar
- 3 garlic cloves, minced
- 1 tablespoon garlic powder
- 1 tablespoon paprika
- 1 tablespoon ground cumin
- 1 tablespoon dried parsley
- 1 tablespoon dried thyme
- 1 tablespoon dried oregano
- 1 teaspoon salt
- ½ teaspoon freshly ground black pepper
- Juice of ½ lemon
- 1 (3-pound) boneless leg of lamb

Directions:
1. In a large bowl, mix together the vinegar, garlic, garlic powder, paprika, cumin, parsley, thyme, oregano, salt, pepper, and lemon juice until well combined—the marinade will turn into a thick paste. Add the leg of lamb and massage the marinade into the meat. Coat the lamb with the marinade and let sit for at least 30 minutes. If marinating for longer, cover and refrigerate.
2. Plug the thermometer into the unit. Insert the Grill Grate and close the hood. Select GRILL, set the temperature to LO, and set the time to 30 minutes. Insert the Smart Thermometer into the thickest part of the meat. Select START/STOP to begin preheating.
3. When the unit beeps to signify it has preheated, place the lamb on the Grill Grate. Select the BEEF/LAMB preset and choose MEDIUM-WELL or according to your desired doneness. Close the hood and cook for 30 minutes.
4. After 30 minutes, which is the maximum time for the LO setting, select GRILL again, set the temperature to LO, and set the time to 30 minutes. Select START/STOP and press PREHEAT to skip preheating. Cook until the Smart Thermometer indicates that the desired internal temperature has been reached.
5. When cooking is complete, remove the lamb from the grill and serve.

Easy Beef Schnitzel

Servings: 1 | Cooking Time: 12 Minutes

Ingredients:
- ½ cup friendly bread crumbs
- 2 tablespoons olive oil
- Pepper and salt, to taste
- 1 egg, beaten
- 1 thin beef schnitzel

Directions:
1. Insert the Crisper Basket and close the hood. Select AIR CRISP, set the temperature to 350ºF, and set the time to 12 minutes. Select START/STOP to begin preheating.
2. In a shallow dish, combine the bread crumbs, oil, pepper, and salt.
3. In a second shallow dish, place the beaten egg.
4. Dredge the schnitzel in the egg before rolling it in the bread crumbs.
5. Put the coated schnitzel in the Crisper Basket. Close the hood and AIR CRISP for 12 minutes. Flip the schnitzel halfway through.
6. Serve immediately.

Hamburger Steak With Mushroom Gravy

Servings: 4 | Cooking Time: 18 Minutes

Ingredients:
- For the hamburger steaks
- 1 cup plain bread crumbs
- 2 tablespoons Worcestershire sauce
- 1 teaspoon onion powder
- 1 teaspoon garlic powder
- 1 large egg
- 1 teaspoon granulated sugar
- 1 teaspoon salt
- ¼ teaspoon freshly ground black pepper
- 1 pound ground beef
- For the mushroom gravy
- 2 cups beef broth
- 4 tablespoons (½ stick) unsalted butter
- 8 ounces white mushrooms, sliced
- 1 tablespoon Worcestershire sauce
- 4 tablespoons all-purpose flour
- Salt
- Freshly ground black pepper

Directions:
1. Insert the Grill Grate and close the hood. Select GRILL, set the temperature to HI, and set the time to 10 minutes. Select START/STOP to begin preheating.
2. While the unit is preheating, in a large bowl, combine the bread crumbs, Worcestershire sauce, onion powder, garlic powder, egg, sugar, salt, and pepper. Add the ground beef in chunks and loosely mix until just combined. Form the mixture into 4 equal-sized patties.
3. When the unit beeps to signify it has preheated, place the beef patties on the Grill Grate. Close the hood and grill for 5 minutes.
4. While the patties are cooking, gather and measure the ingredients for the gravy.
5. After 5 minutes, open the hood and flip the burgers. Close the hood and cook for 5 minutes more.
6. When cooking is complete, use grill mitts to remove the Grill Grate and burgers from the unit.
7. Add the beef broth, butter, mushrooms, and Worcestershire sauce to the Cooking Pot. Select GRILL, set the temperature to HI, and set the time to 8 minutes. Select START/STOP and then press the PREHEAT button to skip preheating. Close the hood and cook for 4 minutes.
8. After 4 minutes, open the hood and stir in the flour. Mix well. Close the hood and cook for 4 minutes more.
9. When cooking is complete, the sauce will be thickened and the butter will be completely melted. Season with salt and pepper. Pour the mushroom gravy over the hamburger steaks and serve.

Smoked Beef

Servings: 8 | Cooking Time: 45 Minutes

Ingredients:

- 2 pounds roast beef, at room temperature
- 2 tablespoons extra-virgin olive oil
- 1 teaspoon sea salt flakes
- 1 teaspoon ground black pepper
- 1 teaspoon smoked paprika
- Few dashes of liquid smoke
- 2 jalapeño peppers, thinly sliced

Directions:

1. Select ROAST, set the temperature to 330ºF, and set the time to 45 minutes. Select START/STOP to begin preheating.
2. With kitchen towels, pat the beef dry.
3. Massage the extra-virgin olive oil, salt, black pepper, and paprika into the meat. Cover with liquid smoke.
4. Put the beef in the pot. Close the hood and ROAST for 30 minutes. Flip the roast over and allow to roast for another 15 minutes.
5. When cooked through, serve topped with sliced jalapeños.

Burnt Ends

Servings: 6 | Cooking Time: 40 Minutes

Ingredients:

- 1 tablespoon garlic powder
- 1 tablespoon sea salt
- 1 tablespoon paprika
- ¼ teaspoon freshly ground black pepper
- 2 pounds pork butt, cut into 1-inch cubes
- ½ cup barbecue sauce
- ¼ cup light brown sugar, packed
- ¼ cup honey
- 4 tablespoons (½ stick) unsalted butter, sliced

Directions:

1. Insert the Cooking Pot and close the hood. Select ROAST, set the temperature to 300°F, and set the time to 20 minutes. Select START/STOP to begin preheating.
2. While the unit is preheating, in a large bowl, combine the garlic powder, salt, paprika, and pepper. Add the pork and toss until generously coated on all sides.
3. When the unit beeps to signify it has preheated, place the pork in the Cooking Pot in a single layer. Close the hood and roast for 10 minutes.
4. After 10 minutes, open the hood and flip the pork cubes. Close the hood and cook for 10 minutes more.
5. At this point, the pork should have a nice char. Place the pork cubes in the center of a large piece of aluminum foil. Add the barbecue sauce, brown sugar, and honey and massage them into the roasted pork. Add the butter, then seal the foil. Place the packet back in the Cooking Pot.
6. Select ROAST, set the temperature to 350°F, and set the time to 20 minutes. Select START/STOP and then press PREHEAT to skip preheating. Close the hood and cook for 20 minutes.
7. When cooking is complete, remove the foil packet. Be careful opening the foil, because the steam will be very hot. The pork should be nicely coated with sauce that has thickened. If you want more char and caramelization of the burnt ends, carefully place the open foil packet back in the Cooking Pot. Select GRILL, set the temperature to HI, and set the time to 10 minutes. Select START/STOP and then press PREHEAT to skip preheating. Close the hood and cook for 10 minutes or until charred to your liking.

Cheesy Beef Meatballs

Servings: 6 | Cooking Time: 18 Minutes

Ingredients:
- 1 pound ground beef
- ½ cup grated Parmesan cheese
- 1 tablespoon minced garlic
- ½ cup Mozzarella cheese
- 1 teaspoon freshly ground pepper

Directions:
1. Insert the Crisper Basket and close the hood. Select AIR CRISP, set the temperature to 400ºF, and set the time to 18 minutes. Select START/STOP to begin preheating.
2. In a bowl, mix all the ingredients together.
3. Roll the meat mixture into 5 generous meatballs. Transfer to the basket.
4. Close the hood and AIR CRISP for 18 minutes.
5. Serve immediately.

Beef And Vegetable Cubes

Servings: 4 | Cooking Time: 17 Minutes

Ingredients:
- 2 tablespoons olive oil
- 1 tablespoon apple cider vinegar
- 1 teaspoon fine sea salt
- ½ teaspoons ground black pepper
- 1 teaspoon shallot powder
- ¾ teaspoon smoked cayenne pepper
- ½ teaspoons garlic powder
- ¼ teaspoon ground cumin
- 1 pound top round steak, cut into cubes
- 4 ounces broccoli, cut into florets
- 4 ounces mushrooms, sliced
- 1 teaspoon dried basil
- 1 teaspoon celery seeds

Directions:
1. Massage the olive oil, vinegar, salt, black pepper, shallot powder, cayenne pepper, garlic powder, and cumin into the cubed steak, ensuring to coat each piece evenly.
2. Allow to marinate for a minimum of 3 hours.
3. Insert the Crisper Basket and close the hood. Select AIR CRISP, set the temperature to 365ºF, and set the time to 12 minutes. Select START/STOP to begin preheating.
4. Put the beef cubes in the Crisper Basket. Close the hood and AIR CRISP for 12 minutes.
5. When the steak is cooked through, place it in a bowl.
6. Wipe the grease from the basket and pour in the vegetables. Season them with basil and celery seeds.
7. Increase the temperature of the grill to 400ºF and AIR CRISP for 5 to 6 minutes. When the vegetables are hot, serve them with the steak.

Bacon Burger Meatballs

Servings: 4 | Cooking Time: 20 Minutes

Ingredients:
- 1 white onion, diced
- 1 pound thick-cut bacon (12 to 16 slices), cooked and crumbled
- 8 ounces cream cheese, at room temperature
- 4 tablespoons minced garlic
- ¼ cup ketchup
- ¼ cup yellow mustard
- ¼ cup gluten-free Worcestershire sauce
- 3 eggs
- 2 pounds ground beef

Directions:
1. In a large bowl, mix together the onion, bacon crumbles, cream cheese, garlic, ketchup, mustard, Worcestershire sauce, and eggs. Add the ground beef and, using your hands, mix the ingredients together until just combined, being careful to not overmix. Form the mixture into 1½- to 2-inch meatballs. This should make 20 to 22 meatballs.
2. Insert the Grill Grate and close the hood. Select GRILL, set the temperature to MED, and set the time to 20 minutes. Select START/STOP to begin preheating.
3. When the unit beeps to signify it has preheated, place the meatballs on the Grill Grate. Close the hood and cook for 10 minutes.
4. After 10 minutes, open the hood and flip the meatballs. Close the hood and cook for 10 minutes more.
5. When cooking is complete, remove the meatballs from the grill and serve.

Italian Sausage And Peppers

Servings: 4 | Cooking Time: 10 Minutes

Ingredients:
- 1 green bell pepper
- 1 large red onion
- 1 pound ground Italian sausage (not links)
- 1 tablespoon garlic, minced
- 2 tablespoons white wine vinegar

Directions:
1. Insert the Cooking Pot and close the hood. Select GRILL, set the temperature to HI, and set the time to 10 minutes. Select START/STOP to begin preheating.
2. While the unit is preheating, cut the bell pepper into strips and slice the red onion.
3. When the unit beeps to signify it has preheated, place the sausage, garlic, and vinegar in the Cooking Pot. Slowly break apart the sausage using a wooden spoon or a spatula. Close the hood and cook for 5 minutes.
4. After 5 minutes, open the hood and stir the sausage. Add the bell pepper and onion. Close the hood and cook for 5 minutes more.
5. When cooking is complete, stir the sausage, pepper, and onion again. Serve.

Peppercorn Beef Tenderloin

Servings: 6 To 8 | Cooking Time: 30 Minutes

Ingredients:
- ¾ cup tricolored peppercorns or black peppercorns, crushed
- 2 garlic cloves, minced
- 2 tablespoons avocado oil
- 1 tablespoon kosher salt
- ¼ cup yellow mustard or horseradish
- 1 (3-pound) beef tenderloin, trimmed

Directions:

1. In a small bowl, combine the crushed peppercorns, garlic, avocado oil, salt, and mustard. Using a basting brush, coat the tenderloin all over with the mustard mixture. Then press the mixture into the meat with your hands.

2. Plug the thermometer into the unit. Insert the Grill Grate and close the hood. Select ROAST, set the temperature to 400°F, then select PRESET. Use the arrows to the right to select BEEF. The unit will default to WELL to cook to a safe temperature. Insert the Smart Thermometer into the thickest part of the loin. Select START/STOP to begin preheating.

3. When the unit beeps to signify it has preheated, place the tenderloin on the Grill Grate. (If the Splatter Shield is touching the tenderloin when you close the hood, use grill mitts to remove the Grill Grate and place the tenderloin in the Cooking Pot instead.) Close the hood and cook until the Smart Thermometer indicates your desired internal temperature has been reached.

4. When cooking is complete, remove the tenderloin and let rest for 10 minutes before slicing and serving.

5. You will want to tuck the thin (tail) end under the center and tie it with kitchen twine or butcher's twine every 2 inches to make a uniform size to get the perfect level of doneness throughout. You can also ask your butcher to tie it for you.

Lamb Rack With Pistachio

Servings: 2 | Cooking Time: 20 Minutes

Ingredients:
- ½ cup finely chopped pistachios
- 1 teaspoon chopped fresh rosemary
- 3 tablespoons panko breadcrumbs
- 2 teaspoons chopped fresh oregano
- 1 tablespoon olive oil
- Salt and freshly ground black pepper, to taste
- 1 lamb rack, bones fat trimmed and frenched
- 1 tablespoon Dijon mustard

Directions:

1. Insert the Crisper Basket and close the hood. Select AIR CRISP, set the temperature to 380°F, and set the time to 12 minutes. Select START/STOP to begin preheating.

2. Put the pistachios, rosemary, breadcrumbs, oregano, olive oil, salt, and black pepper in a food processor. Pulse to combine until smooth.

3. Rub the lamb rack with salt and black pepper on a clean work surface, then place it in the basket.

4. Close the hood and AIR CRISP for 12 minutes or until lightly browned. Flip the lamb halfway through the cooking time.

5. Transfer the lamb to a plate and brush with Dijon mustard on the fat side, then sprinkle with the pistachios mixture over the lamb rack to coat well.

6. Put the lamb rack back to the basket. Close the hood and AIR CRISP for 8 more minutes or until the internal temperature of the rack reaches at least 145°F.

7. Remove the lamb rack from the grill with tongs and allow to cool for 5 minutes before sling to serve.

Servings: 4 | Cooking Time: 52 Minutes

Ingredients:
- 2 teaspoons sesame oil
- 1 teaspoon dried sage, crushed
- 1 teaspoon cayenne pepper
- 1 rosemary sprig, chopped
- 1 thyme sprig, chopped
- Sea salt and ground black pepper, to taste
- 2 pounds pork leg roast, scored
- ½ pound candy onions, sliced
- 4 cloves garlic, finely chopped
- 2 chili peppers, minced

Directions:
1. Select AIR CRISP, set the temperature to 400ºF, and set the time to 52 minutes. Select START/STOP to begin preheating.
2. In a mixing bowl, combine the sesame oil, sage, cayenne pepper, rosemary, thyme, salt and black pepper until well mixed. In another bowl, place the pork leg and brush with the seasoning mixture.
3. Place the seasoned pork leg in a baking pan. Place the pan directly in the pot. Close the hood and AIR CRISP for 40 minutes, or until lightly browned, flipping halfway through. Add the candy onions, garlic and chili peppers to the pan and AIR CRISP for another 12 minutes.
4. Transfer the pork leg to a plate. Let cool for 5 minutes and slice. Spread the juices left in the pan over the pork and serve warm with the candy onions.

Tonkatsu

Servings: 4 | Cooking Time: 10 Minutes Per Batch

Ingredients:
- ⅔ cup all-purpose flour
- 2 large egg whites
- 1 cup panko breadcrumbs
- 4 center-cut boneless pork loin chops (about ½ inch thick)
- Cooking spray

Directions:
1. Spritz the Crisper Basket with cooking spray.
2. Insert the Crisper Basket and close the hood. Select AIR CRISP, set the temperature to 375ºF, and set the time to 10 minutes. Select START/STOP to begin preheating.
3. Pour the flour in a bowl. Whisk the egg whites in a separate bowl. Spread the breadcrumbs on a large plate.
4. Dredge the pork loin chops in the flour first, press to coat well, then shake the excess off and dunk the chops in the eggs whites, and then roll the chops over the breadcrumbs. Shake the excess off.
5. Arrange the pork chops in batches in a single layer in the basket and spritz with cooking spray.
6. Close the hood and AIR CRISP for 10 minutes or until the pork chops are lightly browned and crunchy. Flip the chops halfway through. Repeat with remaining chops.
7. Serve immediately.

SEAFOOD

Chili-lime Shrimp Skewers

Servings: 4 | Cooking Time: 10 Minutes

Ingredients:

- 2 pounds jumbo shrimp, peeled
- 1 tablespoon chili powder
- ¼ teaspoon ground cumin
- ¼ teaspoon dried oregano
- ¼ teaspoon garlic powder
- 2 tablespoons honey
- Juice of 2 limes, divided
- Instant rice, prepared as directed

Directions:

1. Insert the Grill Grate and close the hood. Select GRILL, set the temperature to HI, and set the time to 5 minutes. Select START/STOP to begin preheating.
2. While the unit is preheating, thread 4 or 5 shrimp onto each of 8 skewers, leaving about an inch of space at the bottom. Place the skewers on a large plate.
3. In a small bowl, combine the chili powder, cumin, oregano, and garlic powder. Lightly coat the shrimp with the dry rub. In the same bowl, add the honey and the juice of ½ lime to any remaining seasoning. Mix together.
4. When the unit beeps to signify it has preheated, place 4 shrimp skewers on the Grill Grate. Brush the shrimp with some of the honey mixture. Close the hood and grill for 2 minutes, 30 seconds.
5. After 2 minutes, 30 seconds, open the hood and squeeze the juice of another ½ lime over the skewers and flip. Brush on more honey mixture. Close the hood and cook for 2 minutes, 30 seconds.
6. When cooking is complete, the shrimp should be opaque and pink. Remove the skewers from the grill. Select GRILL, set the temperature to HI, and set the time to 5 minutes. Select START/STOP to begin and press PREHEAT to skip preheating. Repeat steps 4 and 5 for the remaining 4 skewers. When all of the skewers are cooked, serve with the rice.

Crusted Codfish

Servings: 4 | Cooking Time: 8 Minutes

Ingredients:

- 1 cup panko bread crumbs
- 2 tablespoons grated Parmesan cheese
- ¼ cup chopped pistachios
- 4 (4-ounce) frozen cod fillets, thawed
- 4 tablespoons Dijon mustard
- Cooking spray

Directions:

1. Insert the Grill Grate and close the hood. Select GRILL, set the temperature to HI, and set the time to 8 minutes. Select START/STOP to begin preheating.
2. While the unit is preheating, on a large plate, mix together the panko bread crumbs, Parmesan cheese, and pistachios. Evenly coat both sides of the cod fillets with the mustard, then press the fillets on the panko mixture on both sides to create a crust.
3. When the unit beeps to signify it has preheated, spray the crusted fillets with cooking spray and place them on the Grill Grate. Close the hood and grill for 4 minutes.
4. After 4 minutes, open the hood and flip the fillets. Close the hood and cook for 4 minutes more.
5. When cooking is complete, remove the fillets from the grill and serve.

Buttered Lobster Tails

Servings: 6 | Cooking Time: 7 Minutes

Ingredients:

- 6 (4-ounce) lobster tails
- Paprika
- Salt
- Freshly ground black pepper
- 4 tablespoons (½ stick) unsalted butter, melted
- 3 garlic cloves, minced

Directions:

1. Place the lobster tails shell-side up on a cutting board. Using kitchen shears, cut each shell down the center, stopping at the base of the tail. Carefully crack open the shell by sliding your thumbs between the shell and meat and delicately pulling apart. Wiggle, pull, and lift the meat out of the shell. Remove the vein and digestive tract, if present. Rest the meat on top of the shell for a beautiful display.

2. Insert the Grill Grate and close the hood. Select GRILL, set the temperature to HI, and set the time to 7 minutes. Select START/STOP to begin preheating.

3. While the unit is preheating, season the lobster meat with paprika, salt, and pepper.

4. In a small bowl, combine the melted butter and garlic.

5. When the unit beeps to signify it has preheated, place the lobster tails on their shells on the Grill Grate. Close the hood and grill for 4 minutes.

6. After 4 minutes, open the hood and brush the garlic butter on the lobster meat. Close the hood and cook for 3 minutes more.

7. When cooking is complete, the lobster meat will be opaque and the shell will be orangey red. Serve with more melted butter or a sauce of your choice.

Grilled Mahi-mahi Tacos With Spicy Coleslaw

Servings: 4 | Cooking Time: 10 Minutes

Ingredients:

- 1 teaspoon garlic powder
- 1 teaspoon onion powder
- 1 tablespoon paprika
- ¼ teaspoon salt
- 4 (8-ounce) mahi-mahi fillets
- Avocado oil
- Juice of 2 limes, divided
- 1 cup mayonnaise
- 1 tablespoon sriracha
- ⅛ teaspoon cayenne pepper
- ½ head red cabbage, shredded
- 8 (6-inch) corn tortillas

Directions:

1. Insert the Grill Grate and close the hood. Select GRILL, set the temperature to MED, and set the time to 10 minutes. Select START/STOP to begin preheating.

2. While the unit is preheating, in a small bowl, combine the garlic powder, onion powder, paprika, and salt. Place the mahi-mahi fillets on a large plate and rub avocado oil on both sides. Then squeeze the juice of 1 lime on top and generously coat the fillets with the seasoning mix.

3. When the unit beeps to signify it has preheated, place the fillets on the Grill Grate. Close the hood and grill for 8 minutes.

4. While the mahi-mahi is cooking, in a large bowl, combine the mayonnaise, sriracha, cayenne pepper, and the juice of the remaining lime. Add the shredded cabbage to the bowl and stir until combined.

5. After 8 minutes, open the hood and remove the fillets from the grill. Place the tortillas on the Grill Grate. Close the hood to warm them for 2 minutes. Feel free to flip after 1 minute, if desired.

6. Cut the mahi-mahi into ½-inch to 1-inch strips. To assemble the tacos, place the mahi-mahi pieces on the tortillas and dress with the spicy coleslaw mix. Serve.

Shrimp Boil

Servings: 6 | Cooking Time: 10 Minutes

Ingredients:
- 2 tablespoons lemon-pepper seasoning
- 2 tablespoons light brown sugar, packed
- 2 tablespoons minced garlic
- 2 tablespoons Old Bay seasoning
- ¼ teaspoon Cajun seasoning
- ¼ teaspoon paprika
- ¼ teaspoon cayenne pepper
- 1 teaspoon garlic powder
- 1½ cups (3 sticks) unsalted butter, cut into quarters
- 2 pounds shrimp

Directions:
1. Insert the Cooking Pot and close the hood. Select GRILL, set the temperature to MED, and set the time to 10 minutes. Select START/STOP to begin preheating.
2. While the unit is preheating, in a small bowl, combine the lemon pepper, brown sugar, minced garlic, Old Bay seasoning, Cajun seasoning, paprika, cayenne pepper, and garlic powder.
3. When the unit beeps to signify it has preheated, place the butter and the lemon-pepper mixture in the Cooking Pot. Insert the Grill Grate and place the shrimp on it in a single layer. Close the hood and grill for 5 minutes.
4. After 5 minutes, open the hood and use grill mitts to remove the Grill Grate. Place the shrimp in the Cooking Pot. Stir to combine. Close the hood and cook for 5 minutes more.
5. When cooking is complete, open the hood and stir once more. Then close the hood and let the butter set with the shrimp for 5 minutes. Serve.

Tomato-stuffed Grilled Sole

Servings: 6 | Cooking Time: 7 Minutes

Ingredients:
- 6 tablespoons mayonnaise
- 1 teaspoon garlic powder
- 1 (14-ounce) can diced tomatoes, drained
- 6 (4-ounce) sole fillets
- Cooking spray
- 6 tablespoons panko bread crumbs

Directions:
1. Insert the Grill Grate and close the hood. Select GRILL, set the temperature to HI, and set the time to 7 minutes. Select START/STOP to begin preheating.
2. While the unit is preheating, in a small bowl, combine the mayonnaise and garlic powder. Slowly fold in the tomatoes, making sure to be gentle so they don't turn to mush. Place the sole fillets on a large, flat surface and spread the mayonnaise across the top of each. Roll up the fillets, creating pinwheels. Spray the top of each roll with cooking spray, then press 1 tablespoon of panko bread crumbs on top of each.
3. When the unit beeps to signify it has preheated, place the fillets on the Grill Grate, seam-side down. Close the hood and grill for 7 minutes.
4. When cooking is complete, the panko bread crumbs will be crisp, and the fish will have turned opaque. Remove the fish from the grill and serve.

Honey-walnut Shrimp

Servings: 4 | Cooking Time: 8 Minutes

Ingredients:
- 2 ounces walnuts
- 2 tablespoons honey
- 1 egg
- 1 cup panko bread crumbs
- 1 pound shrimp, peeled
- ½ cup mayonnaise
- 1 teaspoon powdered sugar
- 2 tablespoons heavy (whipping) cream
- Scallions, both white and green parts, sliced, for garnish

Directions:

1. Insert the Grill Grate. In a small heat-safe bowl, combine the walnuts and honey, then place the bowl on the Grill Grate and close the hood. Select GRILL, set the temperature to HI, and set the time to 8 minutes. Select START/STOP to begin preheating. After 2 minutes of preheating (set a separate timer), remove the bowl. Close the hood to continue preheating.

2. While the unit is preheating, create an assembly line with 2 large bowls. In the first bowl, whisk the egg. Put the panko bread crumbs in the other bowl. One at a time, dip the shrimp in the egg and then into the panko bread crumbs until well coated. Place the breaded shrimp on a plate.

3. When the unit beeps to signify it has preheated, place the shrimp on the Grill Grate in a single layer. Close the hood and cook for 4 minutes.

4. After 4 minutes, open the hood and flip the shrimp. Close the hood and cook for 4 minutes more.

5. While the shrimp are cooking, in a large bowl, combine the mayonnaise, powdered sugar, and heavy cream and mix until the sugar has dissolved.

6. When cooking is complete, remove the shrimp from the grill. Add the cooked shrimp and honey walnuts to the mayonnaise mixture and gently fold them together. Garnish with scallions and serve.

Garlic Butter Shrimp Kebabs

Servings: 4 | Cooking Time: 10 Minutes

Ingredients:
- 2 tablespoons unsalted butter, at room temperature
- 4 garlic cloves, minced
- 2 pounds jumbo shrimp, peeled
- 1 tablespoon garlic salt
- 1 teaspoon dried parsley

Directions:

1. Insert the Grill Grate. Place the butter and minced garlic in a heat-safe bowl, place the bowl on the Grill Grate, and close the hood. Select GRILL, set the temperature to HI, and set the time to 5 minutes. Select START/STOP to begin preheating. After 1 minute of preheating (set a separate timer), remove the bowl with the butter. Close the hood to continue preheating.

2. While the unit is preheating, place 4 or 5 shrimp on each of 8 skewers, with at least 1 inch left at the bottom. Place the skewers on a large plate. Lightly coat them with the garlic salt and parsley.

3. When the unit beeps to signify it has preheated, place 4 skewers on the Grill Grate. Brush some of the melted garlic butter on the shrimp. Close the hood and grill for 2 minutes, 30 seconds.

4. After 2 minutes, 30 seconds, open the hood and brush the shrimp with garlic butter again, then flip the skewers. Brush on more garlic butter. Close the hood and cook for 2 minutes, 30 seconds more.

5. When cooking is complete, the shrimp will be opaque and pink. Remove the skewers from the grill. Select GRILL, set the temperature to HI, and set the time to 5 minutes. Select START/STOP to begin and press PRE-HEAT to skip preheating. Repeat steps 3 and 4 for the remaining skewers. When all the skewers are cooked, serve.

Servings:12 | Cooking Time: 16 Minutes

Ingredients:

- For the crab cakes
- 1 large egg
- 1 tablespoon Old Bay seasoning
- 1 tablespoon dried parsley
- 1 tablespoon soy sauce
- 1 tablespoon minced garlic
- ¼ cup grated Parmesan cheese
- ½ cup mayonnaise
- ½ cup panko bread crumbs
- 1 pound lump crabmeat
- Avocado oil cooking spray
- For the lemon-garlic aioli
- ½ cup mayonnaise
- 1 teaspoon garlic powder
- Juice of 1 lemon
- ¼ teaspoon paprika

Directions:

1. In a large bowl, whisk the egg, then add the Old Bay seasoning, parsley, soy sauce, garlic, Parmesan cheese, mayonnaise, and panko bread crumbs and mix well. Add the crabmeat and fold it in gently so the crabmeat does not fall apart. Form the mixture into 12 equal-size patties. Place the patties on a large baking sheet and refrigerate for at least 30 minutes.

2. Insert the Grill Grate and close the hood. Select Grill, set the temperature to HI, and set the time to 8 minutes. Select START/STOP to begin preheating.

3. When the unit beeps to signify it has preheated, spray avocado oil on both sides of 6 crab cakes and place them on the Grill Grate. Close the hood and cook for 4 minutes.

4. After 4 minutes, open the hood and flip the crab cakes. Close the hood and cook for 4 minutes more.

5. When cooking is complete, remove the crab cakes from the grill. Select GRILL, set the temperature to HI, and set the time to 8 minutes. Select START/STOP to begin and press PREHEAT to skip preheating. Repeat steps 3 and 4 for the remaining 6 crab cakes.

6. While the crab cakes are cooking, in a small bowl, combine the mayonnaise, garlic powder, lemon juice, and paprika. Feel free to add more lemon or a few dashes of hot sauce to adjust the taste to your liking.

7. When all of the crab cakes are cooked, serve with the sauce.

Lemon-garlic Butter Scallops

Servings: 6 | Cooking Time: 4 Minutes

Ingredients:

- 2 pounds large sea scallops
- Salt
- Freshly ground black pepper
- 3 tablespoons avocado oil
- 3 garlic cloves, minced
- 8 tablespoons (1 stick) unsalted butter, sliced
- Juice of 1 lemon
- Chopped fresh parsley, for garnish

Directions:

1. Insert the Cooking Pot and close the hood. Select GRILL, set the temperature to HI, and set the time to 4 minutes. Select START/STOP to begin preheating.

2. While the unit is preheating, pat the scallops dry with a paper towel and season them with salt and pepper. After 5 minutes of preheating (set a separate timer), open the hood and add the avocado oil and garlic to the Cooking Pot, then close the hood to continue preheating.

3. When the unit beeps to signify it has preheated, use a spatula to spread the oil and garlic around the bottom of the Cooking Pot. Place the scallops in the pot in a single layer. Close the hood and cook for 2 minutes.

4. After 2 minutes, open the hood and flip the scallops. Add the butter to the pot and drizzle some lemon juice over each scallop. Close the hood and cook for 2 minutes more.

5. When cooking is complete, open the hood and flip the scallops again. Spoon melted garlic butter on top of each. The scallops should be slightly firm and opaque. Remove the scallops from the grill and serve, garnished with the parsley.

Lobster Rolls

Servings: 4 | Cooking Time: 7 Minutes

Ingredients:
- ¼ cup mayonnaise
- Juice of ½ lemon
- ¼ teaspoon sea salt
- ⅛ teaspoon freshly ground black pepper
- 1 teaspoon dried parsley
- Dash paprika
- 1 pound frozen lobster meat, thawed, cut into 1-inch pieces
- Unsalted butter, at room temperature
- 4 sandwich rolls, such as French rolls, hoagie rolls, or large hot dog buns
- 1 lemon, cut into wedges

Directions:
1. Insert the Grill Grate and close the hood. Select GRILL, set the temperature to MED, and set the time to 7 minutes. Select START/STOP to begin preheating.
2. While the unit is preheating, in a large bowl, combine the mayonnaise, lemon juice, salt, pepper, parsley, and paprika.
3. When the unit beeps to signify it has preheated, place the lobster meat on the Grill Grate. Close the hood and grill for 4 minutes.
4. While the lobster is cooking, spread the butter on the sandwich rolls.
5. After 4 minutes, open the hood and remove the lobster meat. Set aside on a plate. Place the sandwich rolls on the grill, buttered-side down. Close the hood and grill for 2 minutes.
6. After 2 minutes, open the hood and flip the rolls. Close the hood and cook for 1 minute more.
7. When the bread is toasted and golden brown, remove it from the grill. Add the lobster meat to the mayonnaise mixture and gently fold in until well combined. Spoon the lobster meat into the sandwich rolls. Serve with the lemon wedges.

Orange-ginger Soy Salmon

Servings: 4 | Cooking Time: 12 Minutes

Ingredients:
- ½ cup low-sodium soy sauce
- ¼ cup orange marmalade
- 3 tablespoons light brown sugar, packed
- 1 tablespoon peeled minced fresh ginger
- 1 garlic clove, minced
- 4 (8-ounce) skin-on salmon fillets

Directions:
1. In a large bowl, whisk together the soy sauce, orange marmalade, brown sugar, ginger, and garlic until the sugar is dissolved. Set aside one-quarter of the marinade in a small bowl. Place the salmon fillets skin-side down in the marinade in the large bowl.
2. Insert the Grill Grate and close the hood. Select GRILL, set the temperature to MED, and set the time to 12 minutes. Select START/STOP to begin preheating.
3. When the unit beeps to signify it has preheated, place the salmon fillets on the Grill Grate, skin-side down. Spoon the remaining marinade in the large bowl over the fillets. Close the hood and cook for 10 minutes.
4. After 10 minutes, open the hood and brush the reserved marinade in the small bowl over the fillets. Close the hood and cook for 2 minutes more.
5. When cooking is complete, the salmon will be opaque and should flake easily with a fork. (If you want, you can also use the Smart Thermometer at the end of cooking to check that the internal temperature of the salmon has reached 145°F.) Remove the fillets from the grill and serve.

Halibut With Lemon And Capers

Servings: 4 | Cooking Time: 8 Minutes

Ingredients:

- 4 halibut steaks (at least 1 inch thick)
- Extra-virgin olive oil
- 1 lemon
- 1 cup white wine
- 3 garlic cloves, minced
- 4 tablespoons capers
- 4 tablespoons (½ stick) unsalted butter, sliced

Directions:

1. Insert the Cooking Pot and close the hood. Select GRILL, set the temperature to HI, and set the time to 8 minutes. Select START/STOP to begin preheating.
2. While the unit is preheating, drizzle the fish fillets with olive oil. Cut half the lemon into thin slices and place them on top of the fillets.
3. When the unit beeps to signify it has preheated, place the fillets in the Cooking Pot. Close the hood and cook for 4 minutes.
4. After 4 minutes, open the hood and add the white wine. Close the hood and cook for 2 minutes. After 2 minutes, open the hood and add the garlic, capers, and butter. Squeeze the juice of the remaining ½ lemon over the fish. Close the hood and cook for 2 minutes more.
5. When cooking is complete, open the hood and spoon the sauce over the fish. If the capers have not popped, give about half of them a tap with the spoon to pop them. Stir the sauce and serve with the fillets.

Tilapia With Cilantro And Ginger

Servings: 4 | Cooking Time: 8 Minutes

Ingredients:

- Extra-virgin olive oil
- 4 (8-ounce) tilapia fillets
- 2 tablespoons soy sauce
- 1 teaspoon sesame oil
- 1 tablespoon honey
- 1 tablespoon peeled minced fresh ginger
- ½ cup chopped fresh cilantro

Directions:

1. Insert the Cooking Pot and close the hood. Select GRILL, set the temperature to HI, and set the time to 8 minutes. Select START/STOP to begin preheating.
2. While the unit is preheating, drizzle the fish fillets with olive oil.
3. When the unit beeps to signify it has preheated, place the fillets in the Cooking Pot in a single layer. Close the hood and cook for 6 minutes.
4. While the fish is cooking, in a small bowl, whisk together the soy sauce, sesame oil, honey, ginger, and cilantro.
5. After 6 minutes, open the hood and pour the sauce over the fillets. Close the hood and cook for 2 minutes more.
6. When cooking is complete, remove the fillets from the grill and serve.

Mom's Lemon-pepper Salmon

Servings: 4 | Cooking Time: 8 Minutes

Ingredients:
- ¼ cup mayonnaise
- 4 (4- to 5-ounce) skin-on salmon fillets
- 1 tablespoon lemon-pepper seasoning

Directions:
1. Insert the Grill Grate and close the hood. Select GRILL, set the temperature to MED, and set the time to 8 minutes. Select START/STOP to begin preheating.
2. While the unit is preheating, spread the mayonnaise evenly on the flesh of each salmon fillet. Season with the lemon pepper.
3. When the unit beeps to signify it has preheated, place the fillets on the Grill Grate, skin-side down. Close the hood and cook for 8 minutes.
4. When cooking is complete, the salmon will be opaque and should flake easily with a fork. (If you want, you can also use the Smart Thermometer at the end of cooking to check that the internal temperature of the salmon has reached 145°F.) Remove the salmon from the grill and serve.

Coconut Shrimp With Orange Chili Sauce

Servings:44 | Cooking Time: 16 Minutes

Ingredients:
- For the coconut shrimp
- 2 large eggs
- 1 cup sweetened coconut flakes
- 1 cup panko bread crumbs
- ½ teaspoon salt
- ¼ teaspoon freshly ground black pepper
- 2 pounds jumbo shrimp, peeled
- For the orange chili sauce
- ½ cup orange marmalade
- 1 teaspoon sriracha or ¼ teaspoon red pepper flakes

Directions:
1. Insert the Grill Grate and close the hood. Select GRILL, set the temperature to HI, and set the time to 16 minutes. Select START/STOP to begin preheating.
2. While the unit is preheating, create an assembly line with 2 large bowls. In one bowl, whisk the eggs. In the other bowl, combine the coconut flakes, panko bread crumbs, salt, and pepper. One at a time, dip the shrimp in the egg and then into the coconut flakes until fully coated.
3. When the unit beeps to signify it has preheated, place half the shrimp on the Grill Grate in a single layer. Close the hood and cook for 4 minutes.
4. After 4 minutes, open the hood and flip the shrimp. Close the hood and cook for 4 minutes more. After 4 minutes, open the hood and remove the shrimp from the grill.
5. Repeat steps 3 and 4 for the remaining shrimp.
6. To make the orange chili sauce
7. In a small bowl, combine the orange marmalade and sriracha. Serve as a dipping sauce alongside the coconut shrimp.

Servings: 4 | Cooking Time: 8 Minutes

Ingredients:
- 4 (8-ounce) striped bass fillets
- Extra-virgin olive oil
- 2 (1-inch) pieces fresh ginger, peeled and thinly sliced
- ½ cup soy sauce
- ½ cup rice wine (mirin)
- 2 tablespoons sesame oil
- ¼ cup light brown sugar, packed
- ¼ cup water
- ¼ cup sliced scallions, both white and green parts, for garnish

Directions:
1. Insert the Cooking Pot and close the hood. Select GRILL, set the temperature to HI, and set the time to 8 minutes. Select START/STOP to begin preheating.
2. While the unit is preheating, drizzle the fish fillets with olive oil.
3. When the unit beeps to signify it has preheated, place the fillets in the Cooking Pot in a single layer. Place the ginger slices on top of the fillets. Close the hood and cook for 6 minutes.
4. While the fish is cooking, in a small bowl, whisk together the soy sauce, rice wine, sesame oil, brown sugar, and water until the sugar dissolves.
5. After 6 minutes, open the hood and pour the soy sauce mixture over the fish. Close the hood and cook for 2 minutes more.
6. When cooking is complete, open the hood and remove the fillets from the grill. Garnish with the scallions and serve.

SAUCES, DIPS, AND DRESSINGS

Sauces, Dips, And Dressings

Garlic Lime Tahini Dressing

Servings:1 | Cooking Time: 0 Minutes

Ingredients:
- ⅓ cup tahini
- 3 tablespoons filtered water
- 2 tablespoons freshly squeezed lime juice
- 1 tablespoon apple cider vinegar
- 1 teaspoon lime zest
- 1½ teaspoons raw honey
- ¼ teaspoon garlic powder
- ¼ teaspoon salt

Directions:
1. Whisk together the tahini, water, vinegar, lime juice, lime zest, honey, salt, and garlic powder in a small bowl until well emulsified.
2. Serve immediately, or refrigerate in an airtight container for to 1 week.

Ginger Sweet Sauce

Servings:1 | Cooking Time: 5 Minutes

Ingredients:
- 3 tablespoons ketchup
- 2 tablespoons water
- 2 tablespoons maple syrup
- 1 tablespoon rice vinegar
- 2 teaspoons peeled minced fresh ginger root
- 2 teaspoons soy sauce (or tamari, which is a gluten-free option)
- 1 teaspoon cornstarch

Directions:
1. In a small saucepan over medium heat, combine all the ingredients and stir continuously for 5 minutes, or until slightly thickened.
2. Enjoy warm or cold.

Lemon Dijon Vinaigrette

Servings:6 | Cooking Time: 0 Minutes

Ingredients:
- ¼ cup extra-virgin olive oil
- 1 garlic clove, minced
- 2 tablespoons freshly squeezed lemon juice
- 1 teaspoon Dijon mustard
- ½ teaspoon raw honey
- ¼ teaspoon salt
- ¼ teaspoon dried basil

Directions:
1. Place all the ingredients in a mason jar. Cover and shake vigorously until thoroughly mixed and well emulsified.
2. Serve chilled.

Pico De Gallo

Servings: 2 | Cooking Time: 0 Minutes

Ingredients:
- 3 large tomatoes, chopped
- ½ small red onion, diced
- ⅛ cup chopped fresh cilantro
- 3 garlic cloves, chopped
- 2 tablespoons chopped pickled jalapeño pepper
- 1 tablespoon lime juice
- ¼ teaspoon pink Himalayan salt (optional)

Directions:
1. In a medium bowl, combine all the ingredients and mix with a wooden spoon.

Cashew Vodka Sauce

Servings:3 | Cooking Time: 5 Minutes

Ingredients:
- ¾ cup raw cashews
- ¼ cup boiling water
- 1 tablespoon olive oil
- 4 garlic cloves, minced
- 1½ cups unsweetened almond milk
- 1 tablespoon arrowroot powder
- 1 teaspoon salt
- 1 tablespoon nutritional yeast
- 1¼ cups marinara sauce

Directions:
1. Put the cashews in a heatproof bowl and add boiling water to cover. Let soak for 10 minutes. Drain the cashews and place them in a blender. Add ¼ cup boiling water and blend for 1 to 2 minutes or until creamy. Set aside.
2. In a small saucepan, heat the olive oil over medium heat. Add the garlic and sauté for 2 minutes until golden. Whisk in the almond milk, arrowroot powder, and salt. Bring to a simmer. Continue to simmer, whisking frequently, for about 5 minutes or until the sauce thickens.
3. Carefully transfer the hot almond milk mixture to the blender with the cashews. Blend for 30 seconds to combine, then add the nutritional yeast and marinara sauce. Blend for 1 minute or until creamy.

Creamy Ranch Dressing

Servings: 8 | Cooking Time: 0 Minutes

Ingredients:
- 1 cup plain Greek yogurt
- ¼ cup chopped fresh dill
- 2 tablespoons chopped fresh chives
- Zest of 1 lemon
- 1 garlic clove, minced
- ½ teaspoon sea salt
- ⅛ teaspoon freshly cracked black pepper

Directions:
1. Mix together the yogurt, dill, chives, lemon zest, garlic, sea salt, and pepper in a small bowl and whisk to combine.
2. Serve chilled.

Balsamic Dressing

Servings:1 | Cooking Time: 0 Minutes

Ingredients:
- 2 tablespoons Dijon mustard
- ¼ cup balsamic vinegar
- ¾ cup olive oil

Directions:

1. Put all ingredients in a jar with a tight-fitting lid. Put on the lid and shake vigorously until thoroughly combined. Refrigerate until ready to use and shake well before serving.

Hummus

Servings: 2 | Cooking Time: 0 Minutes

Ingredients:
- 1 can chickpeas, drained and rinsed
- ¼ cup tahini
- 3 tablespoons cold water
- 2 tablespoons freshly squeezed lemon juice
- 1 garlic clove
- ½ teaspoon turmeric powder
- ⅛ teaspoon black pepper
- Pinch of pink Himalayan salt

Directions:

1. Combine all the ingredients in a food processor and blend until smooth.

Cashew Pesto

Servings:1 | Cooking Time: 0 Minutes

Ingredients:
- ¼ cup raw cashews
- Juice of 1 lemon
- 2 garlic cloves
- ⅓ red onion
- 1 tablespoon olive oil
- 4 cups basil leaves, packed
- 1 cup wheatgrass
- ¼ cup water
- ¼ teaspoon salt

Directions:

1. Put the cashews in a heatproof bowl and add boiling water to cover. Soak for 5 minutes and then drain.
2. Put all ingredients in a blender and blend for 2 to 3 minutes or until fully combined.

Cashew Ranch Dressing

Servings: 12 | Cooking Time: 0 Minutes

Ingredients:
- 1 cup cashews, soaked in warm water for at least 1 hour
- ½ cup water
- 2 tablespoons freshly squeezed lemon juice
- 1 tablespoon vinegar
- 1 teaspoon garlic powder
- 1 teaspoon onion powder
- 2 teaspoons dried dill

Directions:

1. In a food processor, combine the cashews, water, lemon juice, vinegar, garlic powder, and onion powder. Blend until creamy and smooth. Add the dill and pulse a few times until combined.

DESSERTS

Pound Cake With Mixed Berries

Servings: 6 | Cooking Time: 8 Minutes

Ingredients:

- 3 tablespoons unsalted butter, at room temperature
- 6 slices pound cake, sliced about 1-inch thick
- 1 cup fresh raspberries
- 1 cup fresh blueberries
- 3 tablespoons sugar
- ½ tablespoon fresh mint, minced

Directions:

1. Insert the Grill Grate and close the hood. Select GRILL, set the temperature to MAX, and set the time to 8 minutes. Select START/STOP to begin preheating.
2. While the unit is preheating, evenly spread the butter on both sides of each slice of pound cake.
3. When the unit beeps to signify it has preheated, place the pound cake on the Grill Grate. Close the hood and GRILL for 2 minutes.
4. After 2 minutes, flip the pound cake and GRILL for 2 minutes more, until golden brown. Repeat steps 3 and 4 for all of the pound cake slices.
5. While the pound cake grills, in a medium mixing bowl, combine the raspberries, blueberries, sugar, and mint.
6. When cooking is complete, plate the cake slices and serve topped with the berry mixture.

Chocolate Coconut Brownies

Servings: 8 | Cooking Time: 15 Minutes

Ingredients:

- ½ cup coconut oil
- 2 ounces dark chocolate
- 1 cup sugar
- 2½ tablespoons water
- 4 whisked eggs
- ¼ teaspoon ground cinnamon
- ½ teaspoons ground anise star
- ¼ teaspoon coconut extract
- ½ teaspoons vanilla extract
- 1 tablespoon honey
- ½ cup flour
- ½ cup desiccated coconut
- Sugar, for dusting

Directions:

1. Select BAKE, set the temperature to 355ºF, and set the time to 15 minutes. Select START/STOP to begin pre-heating.
2. Melt the coconut oil and dark chocolate in the microwave.
3. Combine with the sugar, water, eggs, cinnamon, anise, coconut extract, vanilla, and honey in a large bowl.
4. Stir in the flour and desiccated coconut. Incorporate everything well.
5. Lightly grease a baking pan with butter. Transfer the mixture to the pan.
6. Place the pan directly in the pot. Close the hood and BAKE for 15 minutes.
7. Remove from the grill and allow to cool slightly.
8. Take care when taking it out of the baking pan. Slice it into squares.
9. Dust with sugar before serving.

Lemon Ricotta Cake

Servings: 6 | Cooking Time: 25 Minutes

Ingredients:
- 17.5 ounces ricotta cheese
- 5.4 ounces sugar
- 3 eggs, beaten
- 3 tablespoons flour
- 1 lemon, juiced and zested
- 2 teaspoons vanilla extract

Directions:

1. Select BAKE, set the temperature to 320ºF, and set the time to 25 minutes. Select START/STOP to begin pre-heating.
2. In a large mixing bowl, stir together all the ingredients until the mixture reaches a creamy consistency.
3. Pour the mixture into a baking pan. Place the pan directly in the pot.
4. Close the hood and BAKE for 25 minutes until a toothpick inserted in the center comes out clean.
5. Allow to cool for 10 minutes on a wire rack before serving.

Everyday Cheesecake

Servings: 4 | Cooking Time: 35 Minutes

Ingredients:
- 1 large egg
- 8 ounces cream cheese, at room temperature
- ¼ cup heavy (whipping) cream
- ¼ cup sour cream
- ¼ cup powdered sugar
- 1 teaspoon vanilla extract
- 5 ounces cookies, such as chocolate, vanilla, cinnamon, or your favorite
- 4 tablespoons (½ stick) unsalted butter, melted

Directions:

1. In a large bowl, whisk the egg. Then add the cream cheese, heavy cream, and sour cream and whisk until smooth. Slowly add the powdered sugar and vanilla, whisking until fully mixed.
2. Insert the Cooking Pot and close the hood. Select BAKE, set the temperature to 350°F, and set the time to 35 minutes. Select START/STOP to begin preheating.
3. While the unit is preheating, crush the cookies into fine crumbs. Place them in a 6-inch springform pan and drizzle evenly with the melted butter. Using your fingers, press down on the crumbs to form a crust on the bottom of the pan. Pour the cream cheese mixture on top of the crust. Cover the pan with aluminum foil, making sure the foil fully covers the sides of the pan and tucks under the bottom so it does not lift up and block the Splatter Shield as the air flows while baking.
4. When the unit beeps to signify it has preheated, place the springform pan in the Cooking Pot. Close the hood and cook for 25 minutes.
5. After 25 minutes, open the hood and remove the foil. Close the hood and cook for 10 minutes more.
6. When cooking is complete, remove the pan from the Cooking Pot and let the cheesecake cool for 1 hour, then place the cheesecake in the refrigerator for at least 3 hours. Slice and serve.

Servings: 6 | Cooking Time: 15 Minutes

Ingredients:
- 3 tablespoons milk or dark chocolate chips
- 2 tablespoons thick, hot fudge sauce
- 2 tablespoons chopped dried cherries
- 1 sheet frozen puff pastry, thawed
- 1 egg white, beaten
- 2 tablespoons sugar
- ½ teaspoon cinnamon

Directions:
1. Insert the Crisper Basket and close the hood. Select BAKE, set the temperature to 350°F, and set the time to 15 minutes. Select START/STOP to begin preheating.
2. In a small bowl, combine the chocolate chips, fudge sauce, and dried cherries.
3. Roll out the puff pastry on a floured surface. Cut into 6 squares with a sharp knife.
4. Divide the chocolate chip mixture into the center of each puff pastry square. Fold the squares in half to make triangles. Firmly press the edges with the tines of a fork to seal.
5. Brush the triangles on all sides sparingly with the beaten egg white. Sprinkle the tops with sugar and cinnamon.
6. Put in the Crisper Basket. Close the hood and BAKE for 15 minutes or until the triangles are golden brown. The filling will be hot, so cool for at least 20 minutes before serving.

Fudge Pie

Servings: 8 | Cooking Time: 25 To 30 Minutes

Ingredients:
- 1½ cups sugar
- ½ cup self-rising flour
- ⅓ cup unsweetened cocoa powder
- 3 large eggs, beaten
- 12 tablespoons butter, melted
- 1½ teaspoons vanilla extract
- 1 unbaked pie crust
- ¼ cup confectioners' sugar (optional)

Directions:
1. Select BAKE, set the temperature to 350°F, and set the time to 30 minutes. Select START/STOP to begin preheating.
2. Thoroughly combine the sugar, flour, and cocoa powder in a medium bowl. Add the beaten eggs and butter and whisk to combine. Stir in the vanilla.
3. Pour the prepared filling into the pie crust and transfer to the pot.
4. Close the hood and BAKE for 25 to 30 minutes until just set.
5. Allow the pie to cool for 5 minutes. Sprinkle with the confectioners' sugar, if desired. Serve warm.

Cinnamon-sugar Dessert Chips

Servings: 4 | Cooking Time: 10 Minutes

Ingredients:
- 10 (6-inch) flour tortillas
- 8 tablespoons (1 stick) unsalted butter, melted
- 1 tablespoon cinnamon
- ¼ cup granulated sugar
- ½ cup chocolate syrup, for dipping

Directions:

1. Insert the Grill Grate and close the hood. Select GRILL, set the temperature to HI, and set the time to 10 minutes. Select START/STOP to begin preheating.

2. While the unit is preheating, cut the tortillas into 6 equal wedges. In a large resealable bag, combine the tortillas, butter, cinnamon, and sugar and shake vigorously to coat the tortillas.

3. When the unit beeps to signify it has preheated, add half the tortillas to the Grill Grate. Close the hood and cook for 2 minutes, 30 seconds.

4. After 2 minutes, 30 seconds, open the hood and use a spatula to quickly flip the chips or move them around. Close the hood and cook for 2 minutes, 30 seconds more.

5. After 2 minutes, 30 seconds, open the hood and remove the grilled chips and repeat the process with the remaining tortillas.

6. Serve with the chocolate syrup for dipping.

Sugar-glazed Biscuit Bites

Servings: 8 | Cooking Time: 12 Minutes

Ingredients:
- ⅔ cup all-purpose flour, plus additional for dusting
- ⅔ cup whole-wheat flour
- 2 tablespoons granulated sugar
- 1 teaspoon baking powder
- ¼ teaspoon ground cinnamon
- ¼ teaspoon sea salt
- 4 tablespoons salted butter, cold and cut into small pieces
- ⅓ cup whole milk
- Nonstick cooking spray
- 2 cups powdered sugar
- 3 tablespoons water

Directions:

1. In a large bowl, combine the all-purpose flour, whole-wheat flour, sugar, baking powder, cinnamon, and salt. Add the cold butter pieces, and cut them into the flour mixture using a pastry cutter or a fork, until well-combined and the mixture resembles a course meal. Add the milk to the mixture, and stir together until the dough comes together into a ball.

2. Insert the Crisper Basket and close the hood. Select AIR CRISP, set the temperature to 350°F, and set the time to 12 minutes. Select START/STOP to begin preheating.

3. While the unit is preheating, dust a clean work surface with the all-purpose flour. Place the dough on the floured surface, and knead until the dough is smooth and forms a cohesive ball, about 30 seconds. Cut the dough into 16 equal pieces. Gently roll each piece into a smooth ball.

4. When the unit beeps to signify it has preheated, coat the basket well with cooking spray. Place 8 biscuit bites in the basket, leaving room between each, and spray each with cooking spray. Close the hood and AIR CRISP for 10 to 12 minutes, until golden brown.

5. Meanwhile, in a medium mixing bowl, whisk together the powdered sugar and water until it forms a smooth glaze.

6. Gently remove the bites from the basket, and place them on a wire rack covered with aluminum foil. Repeat step 4 with the remaining biscuit bites.

7. Spoon half the glaze over the bites and let cool 5 minutes, then spoon over the remaining glaze.

Servings:16 | Cooking Time: 8 Minutes

Ingredients:
- 3 tablespoons unsalted butter, at room temperature
- ¼ cup packed brown sugar
- 1 tablespoon honey
- 1 egg white
- ½ teaspoon vanilla extract
- ⅓ cup finely grated carrot
- ½ cup quick-cooking oatmeal
- ⅓ cup whole-wheat pastry flour
- ½ teaspoon baking soda
- ¼ cup dried cherries

Directions:
1. Select BAKE, set the temperature to 350ºF, and set the time to 8 minutes. Select START/STOP to begin pre-heating.
2. In a medium bowl, beat the butter, brown sugar, and honey until well combined.
3. Add the egg white, vanilla, and carrot. Beat to combine.
4. Stir in the oatmeal, pastry flour, and baking soda.
5. Stir in the dried cherries.
6. Double up 32 mini muffin foil cups to make 16 cups. Fill each with about 4 teaspoons of dough. Place the cookie cups directly in the pot.
7. Close the hood and BAKE for 8 minutes, 8 at a time, or until light golden brown and just set. Serve warm.

Chocolate S'mores

Servings: 12 | Cooking Time: 3 Minutes

Ingredients:
- 12 whole cinnamon graham crackers
- 2 chocolate bars, broken into 12 pieces
- 12 marshmallows

Directions:
1. Insert the Crisper Basket and close the hood. Select BAKE, set the temperature to 350ºF, and set the time to 3 minutes. Select START/STOP to begin preheating.
2. Halve each graham cracker into 2 squares.
3. Put 6 graham cracker squares in the basket. Do not stack. Put a piece of chocolate into each. Close the hood and BAKE for 2 minutes.
4. Open the grill and add a marshmallow onto each piece of melted chocolate. Bake for 1 additional minute.
5. Remove the cooked s'mores from the grill, then repeat steps 2 and 3 for the remaining 6 s'mores.
6. Top with the remaining graham cracker squares and serve.

Fresh Blueberry Cobbler

Servings: 6 | Cooking Time: 30 Minutes

Ingredients:

- 4 cups fresh blueberries
- 1 teaspoon grated lemon zest
- 1 cup sugar, plus 2 tablespoons
- 1 cup all-purpose flour, plus 2 tablespoons
- Juice of 1 lemon
- 2 teaspoons baking powder
- ¼ teaspoon salt
- 6 tablespoons unsalted butter
- ¾ cup whole milk
- ⅛ teaspoon ground cinnamon

Directions:

1. In a medium bowl, combine the blueberries, lemon zest, 2 tablespoons of sugar, 2 tablespoons of flour, and lemon juice.
2. In a medium bowl, combine the remaining 1 cup of flour and 1 cup of sugar, baking powder, and salt. Cut the butter into the flour mixture until it forms an even crumb texture. Stir in the milk until a dough forms.
3. Select BAKE, set the temperature to 350ºF, and set the time to 30 minutes. Select START/STOP to begin pre-heating.
4. Meanwhile, pour the blueberry mixture into the baking pan, spreading it evenly across the pan. Gently pour the batter over the blueberry mixture, then sprinkle the cinnamon over the top.
5. When the unit beeps to signify it has preheated, place the pan directly in the pot. Close the hood and BAKE for 30 minutes, until lightly golden.
6. When cooking is complete, serve warm.

Blackberry Chocolate Cake

Servings: 8 | Cooking Time: 22 Minutes

Ingredients:

- ½ cup butter, at room temperature
- 2 ounces Swerve
- 4 eggs
- 1 cup almond flour
- 1 teaspoon baking soda
- ⅓ teaspoon baking powder
- ½ cup cocoa powder
- 1 teaspoon orange zest
- ⅓ cup fresh blackberries

Directions:

1. Select BAKE, set the temperature to 335ºF, and set the time to 22 minutes. Select START/STOP to begin pre-heating.
2. With an electric mixer or hand mixer, beat the butter and Swerve until creamy.
3. One at a time, mix in the eggs and beat again until fluffy.
4. Add the almond flour, baking soda, baking powder, cocoa powder, orange zest and mix well. Add the butter mixture to the almond flour mixture and stir until well blended. Fold in the blackberries.
5. Scrape the batter to a baking pan. Place the pan directly in the pot. Close the hood and BAKE for 22 minutes. Check the cake for doneness: If a toothpick inserted into the center of the cake comes out clean, it's done.
6. Allow the cake cool on a wire rack to room temperature. Serve immediately.

Lemony Blackberry Crisp

Servings: 1 | Cooking Time: 20 Minutes

Ingredients:
- 2 tablespoons lemon juice
- ⅓ cup powdered erythritol
- ¼ teaspoon xantham gum
- 2 cup blackberries
- 1 cup crunchy granola

Directions:

1. Select BAKE, set the temperature to 350ºF, and set the time to 15 minutes. Select START/STOP to begin pre-heating.
2. In a bowl, combine the lemon juice, erythritol, xantham gum, and blackberries. Transfer to a round baking pan and cover with aluminum foil.
3. Place the pan directly in the pot. Close the hood and BAKE for 12 minutes.
4. Take care when removing the pan from the grill. Give the blackberries a stir and top with the granola.
5. Return the pan to the grill and bake at 320ºF for an additional 3 minutes. Serve once the granola has turned brown and enjoy.

Chia Pudding

Servings: 2 | Cooking Time: 4 Minutes

Ingredients:
- 1 cup chia seeds
- 1 cup unsweetened coconut milk
- 1 teaspoon liquid stevia
- 1 tablespoon coconut oil
- 1 teaspoon butter, melted

Directions:

1. Select BAKE, set the temperature to 360ºF, and set the time to 4 minutes. Select START/STOP to begin pre-heating.
2. Mix together the chia seeds, coconut milk, and stevia in a large bowl. Add the coconut oil and melted butter and stir until well blended.
3. Divide the mixture evenly between the ramekins, filling only about ⅔ of the way. Transfer to the pot.
4. Close the hood and BAKE for 4 minutes.
5. Allow to cool for 5 minutes and serve warm.

Orange Cake

Servings: 8 | Cooking Time: 23 Minutes

Ingredients:
- Nonstick baking spray with flour
- 1¼ cups all-purpose flour
- ⅓ cup yellow cornmeal
- ¾ cup white sugar
- 1 teaspoon baking soda
- ¼ cup safflower oil
- 1¼ cups orange juice, divided
- 1 teaspoon vanilla
- ¼ cup powdered sugar

Directions:
1. Select BAKE, set the temperature to 350ºF, and set the time to 23 minutes. Select START/STOP to begin preheating.
2. Spray a baking pan with nonstick spray and set aside.
3. In a medium bowl, combine the flour, cornmeal, sugar, baking soda, safflower oil, 1 cup of the orange juice, and vanilla, and mix well.
4. Pour the batter into the baking pan. Place the pan directly in the pot. Close the hood and BAKE for 23 minutes or until a toothpick inserted in the center of the cake comes out clean.
5. Remove the cake from the grill and place on a cooling rack. Using a toothpick, make about 20 holes in the cake.
6. In a small bowl, combine remaining ¼ cup of orange juice and the powdered sugar and stir well. Drizzle this mixture over the hot cake slowly so the cake absorbs it.
7. Cool completely, then cut into wedges to serve.

Marshmallow Banana Boat

Servings: 4 | Cooking Time: 6 Minutes

Ingredients:
- 4 ripe bananas
- 1 cup mini marshmallows
- ½ cup chocolate chips
- ½ cup peanut butter chips

Directions:
1. Insert the Grill Grate and close the hood. Select GRILL, set the temperature to MEDIUM, and set the time to 6 minutes. Select START/STOP to begin preheating.
2. While the unit is preheating, slice each banana lengthwise while still in its peel, making sure not to cut all the way through. Using both hands, pull the banana peel open like you would a book, revealing the banana inside. Divide the marshmallows, chocolate chips, and peanut butter chips among the bananas, stuffing them inside the skin.
3. When the unit beeps to signify it has preheated, place the stuffed banana on the Grill Grate. Close the hood and GRILL for 4 to 6 minutes, until the chocolate is melted and the marshmallows are toasted.

Apple Pie Crumble

Servings: 4 | Cooking Time: 20 Minutes

Ingredients:
- 3 small apples, such as Honeycrisp, Gala, Pink Lady, or Granny Smith, peeled, cored, and cut into ⅛-inch-thick slices
- ¼ cup granulated sugar
- ½ teaspoon cinnamon
- ½ cup quick-cooking oatmeal
- 4 tablespoons (½ stick) unsalted butter, at room temperature
- ½ cup all-purpose flour
- ½ cup light brown sugar, packed

Directions:
1. Insert the Cooking Pot and close the hood. Select GRILL, set the temperature to LO, and set the time to 20 minutes. Select START/STOP to begin preheating.
2. While the unit is preheating, put the apples in a large bowl and coat with the granulated sugar and cinnamon. In a medium bowl, combine the oatmeal, butter, flour, and brown sugar, stirring to make clumps for the top layer.
3. Place the apples in a 6-inch springform pan in an even layer. Spread the oatmeal topping over the apples.
4. When the unit beeps to signify it has preheated, place the pan in the Cooking Pot. Close the hood and cook for 20 minutes.
5. After 20 minutes, open the hood and remove the pan from the unit. The apples should be soft and the topping golden brown. Serve.

Black And White Brownies

Servings: 1 | Cooking Time: 20 Minutes

Ingredients:
- 1 egg
- ¼ cup brown sugar
- 2 tablespoons white sugar
- 2 tablespoons safflower oil
- 1 teaspoon vanilla
- ⅓ cup all-purpose flour
- ¼ cup cocoa powder
- ¼ cup white chocolate chips
- Nonstick cooking spray

Directions:
1. Select BAKE, set the temperature to 340ºF, and set the time to 20 minutes. Select START/STOP to begin preheating.
2. Spritz a baking pan with nonstick cooking spray.
3. Whisk together the egg, brown sugar, and white sugar in a medium bowl. Mix in the safflower oil and vanilla and stir to combine.
4. Add the flour and cocoa powder and stir just until incorporated. Fold in the white chocolate chips.
5. Scrape the batter into the prepared baking pan.
6. Place the pan directly in the pot. Close the hood and BAKE for 20 minutes, or until the brownie springs back when touched lightly with your fingers.
7. Transfer to a wire rack and let cool for 30 minutes before slicing to serve.

Chocolate Pecan Pie

Servings: 8 | Cooking Time: 25 Minutes

Ingredients:
- 1 unbaked pie crust
- Filling:
- 2 large eggs
- ⅓ cup butter, melted
- 1 cup sugar
- ½ cup all-purpose flour
- 1 cup milk chocolate chips
- 1½ cups coarsely chopped pecans
- 2 tablespoons bourbon

Directions:

1. Select BAKE, set the temperature to 350ºF, and set the time to 25 minutes. Select START/STOP to begin preheating.
2. Whisk the eggs and melted butter in a large bowl until creamy.
3. Add the sugar and flour and stir to incorporate. Mix in the milk chocolate chips, pecans, and bourbon and stir until well combined.
4. Use a fork to prick holes in the bottom and sides of the pie crust. Pour the prepared filling into the pie crust. Place the pie crust in the pot.
5. Close the hood and BAKE for 25 minutes until a toothpick inserted in the center comes out clean.
6. Allow the pie cool for 10 minutes in the basket before serving.

Pecan Pie

Servings: 4 | Cooking Time: 20 Minutes

Ingredients:
- 6 ounces cream cheese, at room temperature
- 4 tablespoons (½ stick) unsalted butter
- 2 large eggs
- 1 teaspoon vanilla extract
- 1 cup light brown sugar, packed
- 1 cup all-purpose flour
- ½ cup pecan halves

Directions:

1. Place the cream cheese and butter in a 7-inch silicone cake pan. Insert the Cooking Pot, place the cake pan in the pot, and close the hood. Select BAKE, set the temperature to 350°F, and set the time to 20 minutes. (If using a metal or glass cake pan, you may need to add 5 to 10 minutes to the baking time.) Select START/STOP to begin preheating. After 5 minutes of preheating (set a separate timer), open the hood and remove the cake pan. (The cream cheese and butter will be melted but not combined.) Close the hood to continue preheating.
2. While the unit is preheating, in a medium bowl, whisk together the eggs, vanilla, brown sugar, and 1½ tablespoons of the melted butter from the cake pan.
3. Transfer the remaining butter and cream cheese from the cake pan to a large bowl and mix to combine. (It may look a little like cottage cheese.) Slowly sift the flour into the bowl. Begin kneading and mixing the dough together with your hands. It may be sticky at first, but continue mixing until it forms into a smooth dough. Place the dough in the cake pan and press it into the bottom and up the sides of the pan to form a piecrust.
4. Pour the filling into the piecrust and top with the pecans.
5. When the unit beeps to signify it has preheated, place the cake pan in the Cooking Pot. Close the hood and bake for 20 minutes.
6. When cooking is complete, the crust edges will be golden brown. Remove the cake pan and let cool to room temperature before slicing and serving.

Servings: 6 To 8 | Cooking Time: 5 Minutes

Ingredients:
- 2 peaches
- 2 firm pears
- 2 plums
- 2 tablespoons melted butter
- 1 tablespoon honey
- 2 to 3 teaspoons curry powder

Directions:
1. Insert the Crisper Basket and close the hood. Select BAKE, set the temperature to 325°F, and set the time to 8 minutes. Select START/STOP to begin preheating.
2. Cut the peaches in half, remove the pits, and cut each half in half again. Cut the pears in half, core them, and remove the stem. Cut each half in half again. Do the same with the plums.
3. Spread a large sheet of heavy-duty foil on the work surface. Arrange the fruit on the foil and drizzle with the butter and honey. Sprinkle with the curry powder.
4. Wrap the fruit in the foil, making sure to leave some air space in the packet.
5. Put the foil package in the basket. Close the hood and BAKE for 5 to 8 minutes, shaking the basket once during the cooking time, until the fruit is soft.
6. Serve immediately.

Classic Pound Cake

Servings: 8 | Cooking Time: 30 Minutes

Ingredients:
- 1 stick butter, at room temperature
- 1 cup Swerve
- 4 eggs
- 1½ cups coconut flour
- ½ cup buttermilk
- ½ teaspoon baking soda
- ½ teaspoon baking powder
- ¼ teaspoon salt
- 1 teaspoon vanilla essence
- A pinch of ground star anise
- A pinch of freshly grated nutmeg
- Cooking spray

Directions:
1. Select BAKE, set the temperature to 320°F, and set the time to 30 minutes. Select START/STOP to begin pre-heating.
2. Spray a baking pan with cooking spray.
3. With an electric mixer or hand mixer, beat the butter and Swerve until creamy. One at a time, mix in the eggs and whisk until fluffy. Add the remaining ingredients and stir to combine.
4. Transfer the batter to the prepared baking pan. Place the pan directly in the pot. Close the hood and BAKE for 30 minutes until the center of the cake is springy. Rotate the pan halfway through the cooking time.
5. Allow the cake to cool in the pan for 10 minutes before removing and serving.

Pineapple And Chocolate Cake

Servings: 4 | Cooking Time: 35 To 40 Minutes

Ingredients:

- 2 cups flour
- 4 ounces butter, melted
- ¼ cup sugar
- ½ pound pineapple, chopped
- ½ cup pineapple juice
- 1 ounce dark chocolate, grated
- 1 large egg
- 2 tablespoons skimmed milk

Directions:

1. Select BAKE, set the temperature to 370ºF, and set the time to 40 minutes. Select START/STOP to begin pre-heating.
2. Grease a cake tin with a little oil or butter.
3. In a bowl, combine the butter and flour to create a crumbly consistency.
4. Add the sugar, chopped pineapple, juice, and grated dark chocolate and mix well.
5. In a separate bowl, combine the egg and milk. Add this mixture to the flour mixture and stir well until a soft dough forms.
6. Pour the mixture into the cake tin and transfer to the grill.
7. Close the hood and BAKE for 35 to 40 minutes.
8. Serve immediately.

Lemon Squares

Servings: 4 | Cooking Time: 35 Minutes

Ingredients:

- 1 cup all-purpose flour
- 8 tablespoons (1 stick) unsalted butter, at room temperature
- ⅓ cup powdered sugar, plus additional for dusting
- 2 large eggs
- ⅔ cup granulated sugar
- ½ teaspoon baking powder
- ¼ teaspoon salt
- Juice of 1 lemon

Directions:

1. Insert the Cooking Pot and close the hood. Select BAKE, set the temperature to 325°F, and set the time to 35 minutes. Select START/STOP to begin preheating.
2. While the unit is preheating, in a large bowl, combine the flour, butter, and powdered sugar. Use your hands to smash and mix until the mixture has a crumbly texture. Transfer the mixture to a 6-inch square pan, using your fingers to press the dough into the bottom of the pan to form a crust.
3. When the unit beeps to signify it has preheated, place the pan in the Cooking Pot. Close the hood and cook for 5 minutes.
4. While the crust is baking, in a small bowl, beat the eggs, then add the sugar, baking powder, salt, and lemon juice and mix until well combined.
5. After 5 minutes, open the hood and pour the lemon filling over the crust. Cover the pan with aluminum foil (use grill mitts), making sure the foil tucks under the bottom of the pan so it does not lift up and block the Splatter Shield as the air flows while baking. Close the hood and cook for 20 minutes.
6. After 20 minutes, open the hood and remove the foil. Close the hood and bake uncovered for 10 minutes more.
7. When cooking is complete, remove the pan and let cool for at least 1 to 2 hours. Dust with additional powdered sugar and serve.

Chocolate Molten Cake

Servings: 4 | Cooking Time: 10 Minutes

Ingredients:
- 3.5 ounces butter, melted
- 3½ tablespoons sugar
- 3.5 ounces chocolate, melted
- 1½ tablespoons flour
- 2 eggs

Directions:
1. Select BAKE, set the temperature to 375ºF, and set the time to 10 minutes. Select START/STOP to begin preheating.
2. Grease four ramekins with a little butter.
3. Rigorously combine the eggs, butter, and sugar before stirring in the melted chocolate.
4. Slowly fold in the flour.
5. Spoon an equal amount of the mixture into each ramekin.
6. Put them in the pot. Close the hood and BAKE for 10 minutes.
7. Put the ramekins upside-down on plates and let the cakes fall out. Serve hot.

Grilled Banana S'mores

Servings: 4 | Cooking Time: 6 Minutes

Ingredients:
- 4 large bananas
- 1 cup milk chocolate chips
- 1 cup mini marshmallows
- 4 graham crackers, crushed

Directions:
1. Insert the Cooking Pot and close the hood. Select GRILL, set the temperature to HI, and set the time to 6 minutes. Select START/STOP to begin preheating.
2. While the unit is preheating, prepare the banana boats. Starting at the bottom of a banana, slice the peel lengthwise up one side and then the opposite side. Pull the top half of the peel back, revealing the fruit underneath, but keeping the bottom of the banana peel intact. With a spoon, carefully scoop out some of the banana. (Eat it or set it aside.) Repeat with each banana. Equally divide the chocolate chips and marshmallows between the banana boats.
3. When the unit beeps to signify it has preheated, place the bananas in the Cooking Pot. Close the hood and cook for 6 minutes.
4. When cooking is complete, remove the bananas from the grill and sprinkle the crushed graham crackers on top. Serve.

Servings: 4 | Cooking Time: 9 Minutes

Ingredients:
- Nonstick baking spray with flour
- 3 tablespoons softened butter
- ⅓ cup plus 1 tablespoon brown sugar
- 1 egg yolk
- ½ cup flour
- 2 tablespoons ground white chocolate
- ¼ teaspoon baking soda
- ½ teaspoon vanilla
- ¾ cup chocolate chips

Directions:
1. Select BAKE, set the temperature to 350°F, and set the time to 9 minutes. Select START/STOP to begin pre-heating.
2. In a medium bowl, beat the butter and brown sugar together until fluffy. Stir in the egg yolk.
3. Add the flour, white chocolate, baking soda, and vanilla, and mix well. Stir in the chocolate chips.
4. Line a baking pan with parchment paper. Spray the parchment paper with nonstick baking spray with flour.
5. Spread the batter into the prepared pan, leaving a ½-inch border on all sides.
6. Place the pan directly in the pot. Close the hood and BAKE for 9 minutes or until the cookie is light brown and just barely set.
7. Remove the pan from the grill and let cool for 10 minutes. Remove the cookie from the pan, remove the parchment paper, and let cool on a wire rack.
8. Serve immediately.

RECIPES

DATE

RECIPES	Salads	Meats	Soups
SERVES	Grains	Seafood	Snack
PREP TIME	Breads	Vegetables	Breakfast
COOK TIME	Appetizers	Desserts	Lunch
FROM THE KITCHEN OF	Main Dishes	Beverages	Dinners

INGREDIENTS

DIRECTIONS

NOTES

SERVING	☆☆☆☆☆
DIFFICULTY	☆☆☆☆☆
OVERALL	☆☆☆☆☆

Date: _____

MY SHOPPING LIST

BASIC KITCHEN CONVERSIONS & EQUIVALENTS

DRY MEASUREMENTS CONVERSION CHART

3 TEASPOONS = 1 TABLESPOON = 1/16 CUP

6 TEASPOONS = 2 TABLESPOONS = 1/8 CUP

12 TEASPOONS = 4 TABLESPOONS = 1/4 CUP

24 TEASPOONS = 8 TABLESPOONS = 1/2 CUP

36 TEASPOONS = 12 TABLESPOONS = 3/4 CUP

48 TEASPOONS = 16 TABLESPOONS = 1 CUP

METRIC TO US COOKING CONVERSIONS

OVEN TEMPERATURES

120 °C = 250 °F

160 °C = 320 °F

180° C = 350 °F

205 °C – 400 °F

220 °C = 425 °F

LIQUID MEASUREMENTS CONVERSION CHART

8 FLUID OUNCES = 1 CUP = 1/2 PINT = 1/4 QUART

16 FLUID OUNCES = 2 CUPS = 1 PINT = 1/2 QUART

32 FLUID OUNCES = 4 CUPS = 2 PINTS = 1 QUART

 = 1/4 GALLON

128 FLUID OUNCES = 16 CUPS = 8 PINTS = 4 QUARTS = 1 GALLON

BAKING IN GRAMS

1 CUP FLOUR = 140 GRAMS

1 CUP SUGAR = 150 GRAMS

1 CUP POWDERED SUGAR = 160 GRAMS

1 CUP HEAVY CREAM = 235 GRAMS

VOLUME

1 MILLILITER = 1/5 TEASPOON

5 ML = 1 TEASPOON

15 ML = 1 TABLESPOON

240 ML = 1 CUP OR 8 FLUID OUNCES

1 LITER = 34 FL. OUNCES

WEIGHT

1 GRAM = .035 OUNCES

100 GRAMS = 3.5 OUNCES

500 GRAMS = 1.1 POUNDS

1 KILOGRAM = 35 OUNCES

US TO METRIC COOKING CONVERSIONS

1/5 TSP = 1 ML

1 TSP = 5 ML

1 TBSP = 15 ML

1 FL OUNCE = 30 ML

1 CUP = 237 ML

1 PINT (2 CUPS) = 473 ML

1 QUART (4 CUPS) = .95 LITER

1 GALLON (16 CUPS) = 3.8 LITERS

1 OZ = 28 GRAMS

1 POUND = 454 GRAMS

BUTTER

1 CUP BUTTER = 2 STICKS = 8 OUNCES = 230 GRAMS = 8 TABLESPOONS

WHAT DOES 1 CUP EQUAL

1 CUP = 8 FLUID OUNCES

1 CUP = 16 TABLESPOONS

1 CUP = 48 TEASPOONS

1 CUP = 1/2 PINT

1 CUP = 1/4 QUART

1 CUP = 1/16 GALLON

1 CUP = 240 ML

BAKING PAN CONVERSIONS

1 CUP ALL-PURPOSE FLOUR = 4.5 OZ

1 CUP ROLLED OATS = 3 OZ 1 LARGE EGG = 1.7 OZ

1 CUP BUTTER = 8 OZ 1 CUP MILK = 8 OZ

1 CUP HEAVY CREAM = 8.4 OZ

1 CUP GRANULATED SUGAR = 7.1 OZ

1 CUP PACKED BROWN SUGAR = 7.75 OZ

1 CUP VEGETABLE OIL = 7.7 OZ

1 CUP UNSIFTED POWDERED SUGAR = 4.4 OZ

BAKING PAN CONVERSIONS

9-INCH ROUND CAKE PAN = 12 CUPS

10-INCH TUBE PAN =16 CUPS

11-INCH BUNDT PAN = 12 CUPS

9-INCH SPRINGFORM PAN = 10 CUPS

9 X 5 INCH LOAF PAN = 8 CUPS

9-INCH SQUARE PAN = 8 CUPS

APPENDIX B : RECIPES INDEX

Printed in Great Britain
by Amazon

46736079R00059